MODERN FIGHTER AIRCRAFT

CLB 2998
This edition published in 1993 by Bramley Books
© 1993 CLB Publishing Ltd, Godalming, Surrey, England
Printed and bound in Spain by Graficromo, S.A.
All rights reserved
ISBN 1-85833-016-5

MODERN FIGHTER AIRCRAFT

JEREMY FLACK

Bramley Books

INTRODUCTION

The first fighter aircraft evolved from the early, flimsy flying machines which had been flying prior to World War I. These were originally flown as observation platforms, being a progression from the balloons which had previously been operated by the military in that role for well over a hundred years.

The Royal Flying Corps was formed in the UK on 13th April 1912 with a nucleus of various aircraft types. The aeroplane was seen by the RFC as the way forward in aerial observation, being free to manoeuvre, as opposed to being tethered or drifting in the wind, as was the case with the balloons.

On the 1st April 1914 the British Admiralty formed the Royal Naval Air Service. It was much more forward thinking than the RFC, in that it also saw the aircraft as an offensive machine and carried out trials, dropping bombs and torpedoes.

The pilots would carry a pistol or rifle with them for self defence should they have to force land on enemy territory, but it was not long before the pistols were used to try to hit pilots of enemy observation aircraft encountered over the front.

In the heat of war the fighter aircraft evolved, with machine guns fitted onto the fuselage or wing to give the pilot greater firepower and a better chance of hitting the enemy. These guns were somewhat primitive, in that they were the standard army issue machine gun bolted onto the airframe. Operated by the pilot, they were difficult to reload and frequently jammed or ran out of ammunition.

The two-seat observation aircraft had a short-lived advantage. When an enemy aircraft was encountered, it enabled the observer to concentrate on hitting the enemy with his pistol or rifle – better than relying on the pilot alone. In time the observer was equipped with a machine gun. It was such a crew of a Voisin of the French *Aviation Militaire* that shot down the first enemy aircraft on 5th October 1914.

The main drawback with pusher aircraft was that, while the observer and thus the gun were at the front, the design always lacked power, whilst with a tractor type the observer was positioned in the rear, so he could only fire at aircraft which were attacking. Forward firing guns were still required.

Various attempts were made to improve the effectiveness of the guns, including firing through the propeller arc. This improved the aiming and reloading dramatically. Initially deflectors were fitted to the propeller blades to prevent them being reduced to splinters. The Fokker E.III was the first aircraft to be fitted with a synchronised machine gun with an interrupter preventing the gun from firing when the blade was directly in front of it. It could, indeed, be said that the Fokker E.III was the first true fighter aircraft, and for nearly a year it provided the Germans with air superiority.

Advances in aircraft design, engine power and armament meant that new types evolved and current ones became obsolete in a very short space of time. As a result the advantage held by each side continually changed as newer, more successful types were introduced.

A number of successful names evolved, including the Nieuport Scout, Airco DH.2, and RAE FE.2b operated by the RFC, while the Halberstadt D.II and the Albatross D.I were being built by the Germans. The Albatross introduced the fitting of double machine guns, and it was with this fighter aircraft that one of the German pilots – Baron Manfred, Freiherr von Richthofen – achieved fame as the legendary Red Baron. He was later credited with a total of eighty victories before he was killed flying a Fokker Dr.1 Triplane on 21st April 1918. Richthofen commanded the first real fighter squadron, *Jagdstaffel (Jasta) 2,* which initially formed in August 1918 under the command of another ace, Oswald Boelcke. It was during this period that real fighter aircraft evolved, linking design, manoeuvrability, speed and armament together with tactics.

On 21st May 1917, 21 Gotha G-IV of the Imperial German Army took off from occupied Belgium for the first air raid on London. For various reasons the aircraft did not find their designated target, and this resulted in nearly five tons of bombs being dropped on Folkestone. Although over 40

Fokker E.III Eindekker

Gloster Gladiator

fighters were launched the British defences had been caught out and all the intruders escaped. This attack was followed by several others, including two against London, which caused similar embarrassment for the fighter squadrons. The result was an investigation and report by Jan Christian Smuts. He recommended that a London Air Defence Area be established, with a ring of anti-aircraft guns and fighters around the capital, which proved successful. He also recommended the creation of a strategic bombing force.

The introduction of the RAE SE.5a and the Sopwith Camel in 1917 marked the beginning of British air superiority, despite further advances in German types such as the Fokker D.VII.

At the end of the war the aircraft industry faced decimation. Production had been flat out for many years and numerous companies had sprung up. Suddenly demand from the military was nil, and with vast numbers of surplus aircraft flooding onto the civil market demand from this sector was negligible. Outstanding contracts were cancelled, resulting in many companies disappearing as quickly as they had been formed.

Due to the lack of resources, development of the fighter during the '20s was slow. It remained reliant on the fabric and wooden biplane configuration to which progressively more powerful engines were attached. The Schneider Trophy races probably caused the greatest advance in aircraft design in this period.

R.J.Mitchell designed the S.5 seaplane which took first and second place at the 1927 Schneider Trophy race held in Venice. The winning aircraft flew at an average speed of 281.65 mph. By 1931 the winning S.6B achieved 340.08 mph, at a time when most fighters were only capable of 200 mph.

An Italian, Giulio Douhet, produced a paper in 1927, *The Command of the Air*, which described his theories that aircraft held the winning hand in a future war by holding command of the air. This would be achieved by a massive onslaught to enemy airfields, anti-aircraft gun positions and aircraft factories. These huge formations would also overwhelm any fighters launched, and once all were eliminated would enable the bomber force systematically to hit targets until the enemy would be quickly forced to surrender, with minimal loss of life. While this theory did not prove itself during the Second World War it certainly sounds familiar to events during the Gulf War.

The '30s saw the rumblings of impending troubles around Europe but fighters were given second place to bombers on the list of priorities. In 1934 an Air Ministry specification (F5/34) was issued for a fighter to replace both the Gloster Gauntlet, which was then being built, and the newly-ordered Gladiator biplane. This specification resulted in Sydney Camm's Hawker Hurricane and R.J. Mitchell's Supermarine Spitfire, which entered service in 1937 and 1938 respectively. Meanwhile, the emerging Nazi Party had already started to develop its weaponry with the Heinkel He-51 fighter, which was ordered in 1933 in contravention of the Treaty of Versailles. The design, by Willi Messerschmitt, of the Bf. 108, a two-seat monoplane, provided the basis of the Bf.109 fighter which first flew in September 1935. Like the Spitfire it remained in production right through the war in various marks as development progressed.

The Bristol Blenheim entered service with the RAF in 1937. This was a bomber which was privately funded by Lord Rothermere, and on a test flight in 1935 it flew at 307 mph, 50 mph faster than the Gladiator fighter, of which the first delivery was still awaited.

The year 1937 also saw the entry into RAF service of the Hawker Hurricane, and the Spitfire followed a year later. At a time of growing tension these two fighters emerged to become the cornerstone of the defence of the UK. In September 1939 only 35 fighter squadrons existed in the UK against the estimated 53 that would be required for the country's defence. Amongst these 35 there were still Gauntlets and large numbers of the Gladiator biplanes.

The North American P-51 Mustang was originally designed to meet an RAF specification and entered service with the RAF in May 1942. Its potential was soon recognised by the USAAF and it was ordered in prolific numbers.

As the war progressed a large number of fighter aircraft took on the dual role of fighter-bombers and took part in ground attack operations. They would often be fitted with heavier calibre cannon and were also fitted with racks for carrying bombs.

The introduction of the jet marked a leap forward in the fighter's capabilities. The first flight of the German Heinkel He.178 in August 1939 enabled the design of a new fighter to proceed. On the 18th June 1942 the prototype of the Me.262 fighter took to the air. The pair of Junkers Jumo 004 turbojets propelled the Me.262 up to 540 mph at 23,000 feet. This was over 70 mph faster than the fastest propeller driven aircraft of the time. The Meteor was the RAF's first jet fighter but did not take to the air until March 1943. It entered service in July 1944 and was used to intercept the V-1 flying bombs. It was over 100 mph slower than the Me.262 and had a problem with range, so it was not deployed to fly over Germany. The US produced the F-80, and this took to the air in January 1944, but was too late to be deployed to Europe to combat the small quantities of Me.262 which harassed the piston-engined fighters and bombers.

In 1950 the Korean War initially saw the North Korean Yak-7 and Yak-9s pitted against F-51 Mustangs and F-82 Twin Mustangs. To these were added the F-80C Shooting Star. This became the first American jet fighter to destroy an enemy aircraft when, on 27th June, Captain Raymond Schillereff shot down a North Korean Il-10. The Royal Navy provided the piston-engined Sea Fury operating from a carrier for the UN force while the Royal Australian Air Force provided Meteor F.8s. The US Navy was well equipped with jet fighters, first with the Grumman F-9F Panther and later with the Douglas F-3D Skyknight.

The United Nations forces were able quickly to despatch the North Korean Air Force. For a while they had complete air superiority, enabling bombers to strike without any opposition. On November 1st this changed when a flight of Mustangs had a narrow escape from six Chinese Air Force MiG-15s. On the 8th a raid by B-29s against the city of Sinuiju encountered another flight of six MiGs. Fortunately the B-29s were being escorted by F-80s, and during the ensuing dog fight Lieutenant Russell Brown became the first jet pilot to shoot down an enemy jet aircraft.

The impressive Soviet MiG-15 was at that time superior in most respects to the jets operated by the US forces. Meanwhile the North American Company had been producing the F-86 Sabre, which was deployed to Korea in December 1950. Flying in an area known as MiG Alley, the Sabres, larger and heavier than the MiGs, struggled to hold their own. It was not until the introduction of the F-86F Sabre, which had an increased power plant that the performances became matched. By the end of the conflict the two Wings comprising 75 Sabres

North American P-51 Mustang

Supermarine Spitfire XVI & Messerschmitt BF.109G

had flown over 75,000 sorties compared with over 40,000 by a force of approximately 850 MiGs. A total of 757 MiGs were confirmed as having been destroyed against 103 Sabres lost. A fine testimony to the training and skill of both ground staff and aircrews.

The introduction of the Soviet MiG put the RAF at a disadvantage and resulted in the supply of the North American F-86 Sabre, until the short lived Swift and successful Hunter entered service. The Hawker Hunter proved to be a popular fighter/ground-attack aircraft, with over 1,900 being built for a total of 12 countries.

The tactics used during the Korean War were based on those of WWII, with four aircraft in loose formation and split into pairs comprising a leader and a wingman. The new generation of aircraft, all capable of flying at closing speeds in the region of 700-800 mph, but with onboard radar having a range of only 15 miles and cannon with only a close range capability, meant that the fighter pilot now had only a couple of seconds during which he could hit the target. If the target was a bomber and had fighter cover it was unlikely that he would get a second chance. To improve the effectiveness of the fighter the F-86D Sabre was fitted with 24 Mighty Mouse rockets. These were 70mm unguided missiles which, when launched at a range of 1500 yards, would have a kill probability of around 60 per cent.

It was the introduction of the air-to-air missile which changed the role of the fighter to an interceptor. While most fighters still carry a cannon, the future of the fighter was evolving into a missile launching platform. Since then great efforts have been made in developing the increasingly more sophisticated air-to-air missile.

1953 saw the first of the US Century Series of fighters, commencing with the F-100 Super Sabre. This was the first fighter capable of sustained Mach 1. Out of sequence, the F-102 Delta Dagger was probably the first true interceptor. It was designed from the outset to carry three AIM-4F Falcon air-to-air missiles fitted with Semi-Active Radar Homing (SARH) heads, plus three AIM-4G heat-seeking heads. The F-102 was rapidly superseded by the F-106 Delta Dart, which became part of a package of ground controllers and radar to provide air defence for the whole of the USA. In addition to the Falcon missiles the F-106 could carry an AIR-2A Genie, which had a range of five miles and was designed to position a 1.5 kiloton nuclear warhead into the middle of an enemy formation.

At this time the French were operating the Mystere IV and Super Mystere, and they had a requirement for an all-weather, air-superiority fighter which could reach 60,000ft in six minutes. French manufacturer Dassault built and flew the prototype Mirage III in March 1956. This was the beginning of the highly-successful Mirage family of aircraft which are still in production today.

In the meantime the Soviets had developed the Mig-15 into the MiG-17 and MiG-19. All three types were exported widely to all Warsaw Pact partners as well as to many other countries. China built licensed copies of the MiG-17 as the

Hawker Hunter F.6

Shenyang F-4 and an unlicensed copy of the MiG-19 as the F-6. Considerable numbers of these aircraft remain in service throughout the world.

The first use of the air-to-air missile was during an incident in 1958 between Communist and Nationalist China, when four MiG-15s were shot down in disputed airspace by Sabres.

In 1959 the Soviet Air Force received first deliveries of the MiG.21. This aircraft has been sold in even larger numbers than the previous MiG types and is still widely used.

Introduced in 1958, the F-105 Thunderchief followed a similar role to the of the F-100 which, although conceived as a fighter, saw much of its active service as a fighter-bomber, especially in Vietnam.

In an attempt to rationalise aircraft types and roles the USAF drew up a requirement for an aircraft which was to be capable of Mach 2.5, able to act as escorting fighter, interceptor and bomber, with Short Take Off and Landing (STOL) performance. The US Navy also required an air-superiority fighter to operate from its carriers. The answer was the General Dynamics F-111. Eventually the Navy requirement was dropped. By this time the aircraft was some 77 feet long and weighed over 100,000lbs. It entered service as the first

operational swing-wing aircraft with a role as a strike aircraft.

The 27th of May 1958 saw the first flight of the McDonnell XF4H-1 Phantom II. This aircraft was designed as a carrier-borne air defence and tactical strike aircraft for the USMC and USN. As a fighter it was armed with a combination of AIM-7 Sparrow and AIM-9 Sidewinder AAMs. As a strike aircraft it could carry 16,000lbs of stores. Flight trials proved the Phantom to be of great potential and McDonnell embarked on a programme of breaking numerous world records to establish the aircraft firmly in front of all other types. The result was that the Phantom was demonstrated as being in a class of its own. With the backing of the US Government McDonnell embarked on selling the aircraft overseas. In addition to those for the USMC and USN, orders were received from the USAF in various marks. Subsequently, numerous countries purchased the all-rounder, which was used as a fighter, bomber, reconnaissance and radar suppressor amongst many roles. A total of 5,057 aircraft were delivered by McDonnell to various customers throughout the world, including substantial numbers to Germany and the UK. Additional licence-production aircraft were built in Japan.

Over thirty years later the Phantom is now in decline, with

Aerospace Sea Harriers on HMS *Hermes* and HMS *Invincible*. These two ships, together with two frigates and two RFAs also carried 45 helicopters between them. These comprised of Westland Sea King, Wessex, Lynx and Gazelle to satisfy a variety of roles.

RAF Harriers and RN Sea Harriers were flown to Ascension using the Victor tankers. Some remained at Ascension to provide air defence until replaced by Phantoms, while others were flown onto the *Atlantic Conveyor* for subsequent transfer to HMS *Hermes* and *Invincible*. Also aboard the *Atlantic Conveyor* were additional RN Wessex and Lynx helicopters, plus RAF Chinooks. Disaster struck the ship when it was attacked by a pair of Argentinian Super Etendards which fired their Exocet missiles. Fortunately the Harriers, Sea Harriers and one Chinook had already left, but the rest, plus all the other equipment, were lost.

At the end of the conflict the Harriers and Sea Harriers had accounted for the majority of the 117 Argentinian aircraft/helicopters listed as 'destroyed' or 'probably destroyed' by the Ministry of Defence for the loss of just 10 of their own plus 23 helicopters. During this conflict the Royal Navy Sea Harrier FRS.1s provided fighter cover while the RAF Harriers undertook the ground attack missions. Both aircraft carried the Sidewinder air-to-air missile and both scored victories when encountering Argentinian opposition.

One of the lessons learned from the Falklands Conflict was that the RN loss of the AEW aircraft had cost them dearly. When it had conventional carriers the AEW cover was provided by the Gannet, but these could not be operated by the current generation of ramp-decked carriers. With the carriers planned for North Atlantic or European waters operation AEW coverage was to have been provided by land-based aircraft. To try to rectify this situation Westland rushed through design and production for a variant of the Sea King fitted with AEW.

At this time the Lightning force was being reduced and replaced by the multi-role Phantoms. And the introduction of the Tornado in January 1982 saw the Phantom gradually being replaced in turn. Initially the strike GR.1 entered service with the RAF, to be joined by the ADV or fighter variant. The first Tornado deliveries were designated F.2 and later superseded by the F.3. As delivery progressed the Lightnings were finally withdrawn. Four years later the same is happening to the Phantoms. To assist the RAF fighter force a squadron of Shackletons have provided the airborne early warning cover while awaiting the new generation AEW type. The arrival of the Boeing Sentry AEW.1 in 1990 has resulted in the withdrawal of the world's last front-line piston-engined aircraft and greatly increased the effectiveness of the RAF's fighter force.

In addition to the Tornado F.3, which is a pure fighter, a number of the strike and training aircraft have a fighter capability to a greater or lesser degree. The Tornado GR.1 and Harrier GR.3 and GR.5 have been seen in recent years fitted with Sidewinders. In addition, modifications were made to a number of Hawks, which brought them up to a T.1A standard and gave them an air defence role, for which they were fitted with two Sidewinder missiles. During the Gulf War the Jaguars were fitted with over-wing pylons to which the Sidewinders were fitted.

The Gulf War was a classic example of air power proving the decisive factor in a conflict. Within 38 hours of the order being given, a USAF F-15 Squadron had deployed and was operational in Saudi Arabia. Within four days five combat squadrons and an Airborne Warning And Control System

only a fraction of those purchased for US forces still being flown. However, airforces throughout the Western world still operated them in considerable numbers.

The RAF ordered the Lightning to replace the Javelin. This was the RAF's introduction to a true supersonic fighter. Entering service in 1959, the Lightning has a Mach 2 capability and an initial climb rate of 50,000 feet per minute. Unfortunately it only found limited success in the form of overseas orders. The McDonnell F-4 Phantom was introduced into RAF service to replace the Hunter, and it was initially used in a ground attack and reconnaissance role, but it was later to be employed to augment the Lightning force.

During the early 1980s British Forces were contracting, and the Government's overseas commitments declined. It was progressively becoming geared to meeting only its NATO role, which was to counter the threat from the Soviet Union and Eastern Europe. The arrival of Argentinian scrap merchants on South Georgia, followed by Argentinian Forces on the Falkland Islands – a Sovereign territory 8,000 miles away from the UK – posed a real problem. Ascension provided an air head on Wideawake Island, but this was still 3,900 miles away from the Falklands.

The Royal Navy began despatching the Task Force on 5th April 1982. The only fixed-wing aircraft were the 20 British

English Electric Lightning F.6

contingent were in place. By the end of the conflict 25 fighter squadrons had been flown directly to the Gulf with the assistance of air-to-air refuelling.

Right from the start strike aircraft hit primary targets, breaking down the Iraqi command structure. The Iraqi Air Force initially launched some of its fighters but they were totally overwhelmed, both in terms of quantities of aircraft and qualities of aircrew. Virtually every Iraqi mission ending with aircraft loss and, together with the heavy pounding that all airfields were suffering from the Allied strike aircraft and bombers, many surviving aircraft fled to take refuge in neighbouring Iran. Soon after the Allied forces had broken the back of the Iraqi Air Defence the attack on the ground forces began, and the air strikes proved so successful that by the time the ground war commenced much of the Iraqi Army was waiting to surrender.

Looking into the future, the RAF are expecting to start taking deliveries of the European Fighter Aircraft (EFA) from 1996 onwards. The EFA has combined part of the aircraft industries of Germany, Italy, Spain and the UK to produce the next generation of fighter for their respective air forces. It will be interesting to see how this progresses. In the US the Lockheed YF-22 prototype has been selected as the next generation fighter to replace the F-15.

Looking further into the future, the US Brilliant Pebbles is planned to provide the ultimate as the space-based element of the Strategic Defence Initiative (SDI), with the Global Protection Against Limited Strikes (GPALS) system. This system comprises a constellation of space-based kinetic 'hit to kill' interceptors that remain on standby until activated by a ground-based command centre. The system comprises a metre-long interceptor in a life jacket, which will provide power while on standby, attitude control, surveillance, communications and protection. Once activated, the Brilliant Pebbles system will sense and intercept ballistic missiles. It has been designed to provide a global surveillance capability and to attack missiles in their boost and post-boost phase of a missile attack.

Back to the present, the role of the pure fighter aircraft is to protect one's own airspace. This may be a matter of patrolling a sector of such airspace in readiness; it may involve being scrambled to meet and visually investigate an unidentified return on radar; it might even be to intercept a target and fire on it as soon as it is within range. For these roles the fighter will be armed with air-to-air missiles (AAM) and usually a cannon.

The pure fighter is an expensive item, and the size of a fighter force will depend on a Government's priorities and the budget available. The number of fighters available can, however, be extended by purchasing multi-role aircraft or simply by fitting AAMs to existing combat, or even training, types of aircraft. A strike aircraft is obviously vulnerable if its only defence is a cannon. Fit an AAM and it will have a much better chance.

The ideal fighter is one that is optimised for its role of destroying another aircraft. But it may also be important that it is able to intercept, and then destroy. There can be a difference. A lower performance aircraft is still capable of firing an AAM, but its speed may well be relatively slow, rendering it less capable of interception. On the credit side, such an aircraft may be a fraction of the cost of a high-performance model, and so could be deployed in greater numbers, whilst also filling a role in normal peacetime operations.

Thus the fighter has become a less than clear aircraft type. The most advanced air forces will certainly employ fighter aircraft – the USAF has the F-15 and the F-16 – but they will also be able to load bombs on them. Additionally, aircraft of other types may be capable of being used as fighters in times of tension. The RAF, for instance, can fit Sidewinder AAMs onto their Hawk T.1A training aircraft. Some countries may well not be able to afford the expensive luxury of a pure fighter and so a multi-role aircraft will be purchased. The Bangladesh Air Wing uses the Shenyang F-6 as its fighter as well as its strike aircraft: with AAMs it is a fighter; with bombs it is a strike aircraft.

Although the definition of a fighter aircraft has become clouded, for the purposes of this book, insofar as it deals with the present day, I have taken a fighter to mean an aircraft to which an AAM is fitted. This has widened the scope considerably, and it would now be impossible to include every type. I have tried, however, to include a reasonable cross section of those aircraft which are current or around the corner. I have also included a couple of extreme cases: the RAF Nimrod MR.2s, for example, were fitted with four Sidewinder AAMs during the Falklands War, for protection when they were on patrol and when no traditional fighter cover was available. Had they encountered an Argentinian aircraft, no doubt they would have given a good account of themselves.

Lockheed YF-22 prototype 6807

RIGHT: *In the deep Cold War era countries fell into one of three categories for their military hardware supplies and, more importantly, aid. These were pro-West, pro-East or non-Aligned. In recent years this classification has become blurred. Here we have a formation of the Egyptian Air Force which had traditionally been pro-East and equipped with Soviet weaponry, including MiG fighters. Historical tensions have dictated a strong Egyptian air defence, but the waning of relations with Moscow in the mid '70s resulted in the closing of this channel of supplies. The Egyptians then sought assistance from the West and this formation over the pyramids illustrates the result.*

The formation is led by an Egyptian Air Force F-4E Phantom followed by an F-16 and Mirage 5 from the new era. Continuing down the echelon are the previously supplied MiG-21 and MiG-17. The latter would now be used for ground attack, although it still has a limited fighter role bearing in mind its age. The formation is completed by an F-15 Tomcat, A-7 Corsair II and A-6 from a visiting US Navy aircraft carrier during a co-operation exercise.

RIGHT: *The Chilean Air Force is another operator of the Hawker Hunter, of which a total of 1,985 were built. Demand continued after production finished in 1966 and as a result some 700 airframes were refurbished for re-sale by British Aerospace.*

These three Hunter FGA.71s plus a single FR.71A (2nd aircraft) are from Grupo No. 8 of the Chilean Air Force.

RIGHT: *The Hawker Hunter first flew on 20th July 1951 and it proved a highly successful ground attack aircraft. In RAF service it replaced the Gloster Meteor and has served in the fighter, ground attack, and still remains in the training role. In addition to the RAF and Royal Navy, the Hunter has been operated by numerous countries in its various roles. One of the biggest operators has been the Swiss Air Force, which ordered a total of 160 new and refurbished airframes.*

This Hunter F.58 is armed with an AIM-9 Sidewinder in addition to its 20mm cannon. The markings on the nose indicate that it is also flown by the national aerobatics team – the Patrouille Suisse.

LEFT: *The Blackburn Buccaneer was originally designed as a low-level strike aircraft for the Royal Navy. It first flew on 30th April 1958. Twenty evaluation aircraft were initially ordered, followed by 40 of the production S.1. A further 84 S.2s were ordered for the RN, plus – the only export order – 16 S.50s for the SAAF. With the demise of the RN carriers in 1969, the surviving S.2s were transferred to the RAF, to which a further 43 new aircraft were added. By this time high-level attack was considered unacceptable, with widespread use of Surface to Air Missiles (SAM) in an East-West conflict, and aircraft were therefore required to fly at low-level in the shadow of ground features to avoid detection by radar. This was the type of flying that the Buccaneer was designed for and at which it excelled. Buccaneers of 208 Sqn are illustrated here and two can be seen refuelling from a VC.10 K.3 of 101 Sqn.*

RIGHT: *RAF Buccaneer S.2Bs were deployed from their base at RAF Lossiemouth in Scotland and flown direct to the Gulf with the assistance of air-to-air refuelling. These three Buccaneers were photographed over the Mediterranean Sea en route to the Gulf.*

BELOW: *Buccaneer S.2Bs of 12 Sqn in the standard grey-green camouflage and the newly introduced light grey scheme. The nearest aircraft is carrying a practice bomb pod while the other Buccaneer is fitted with the Pave Spike laser target designator used with success in the Gulf, as well as an inert Sidewinder training missile.*

RIGHT: *Once in the Gulf, the role of the Buccaneers from 12 Sqn was to provide laser designation for the Tornado GR.1s for which they used the Pave Spike system.*

During the Gulf War – Operation Granby to the British military and Desert Shield/Storm to the US – the normal pattern for Buccaneer operations was for a pair of three ship formations comprising 1 Buccaneer to 2 Tornado GR.1s. Over the target the Buccaneer would illuminate the target with the laser designator, enabling the Tornados to release their Laser Guided Bombs (LGB) and being assured of a high hit rate. Later into the conflict the Buccaneers also carried LGB. During the 25 days that the Buccaneers were deployed they flew 678.5 hours on 218 missions.

LEFT: *In keeping with military aviation tradition, the Buccaneers received nose art to record the number of missions flown during Desert Storm and to provide good luck charms. These contributed to maintaining a high crew morale. This particular illustration would appear to hark back to the naval ancestry of the Buccaneer. The bombs reflect the number of missions flown with Tornados, while the red one indicates that the LGBs were actually dropped by the Buccaneer. The aircraft silhouette indicates that one of the bombs dropped destroyed an Iraqi An-12 transport on the ground.*

RIGHT AND BELOW: *The British Aerospace Hawk T.1 first flew on 21st August 1974. It was designed as an advanced trainer and weapons trainer for the RAF. For the latter role it is fitted with three pylons, although it can be modified for a five-pylon configuration. One hundred and seventy-five were ordered for the RAF as an advanced trainer based at RAF Valley. Weapon training is flown from RAF Chivenor, where it is normally fitted with a 30mm Aden gun and a pair of practice bomb pods.*

In January 1983 an order was placed with BAe to modify 89 Hawk T.1s to enable them to carry a pair of Sidewinders for the local air defence role. The aircraft were then designated Hawk T.1A and provided the RAF with additional fighter strength when required without detracting from their peacetime training role.

Orders for the Hawk have included 50 Mk.51s for Finland, 12 Mk.52s for Kenya, 20 Mk.53s for Indonesia, 13 Mk.60s for Zimbabwe, 20 Mk.60s for South Korea, 24 Mk.61s for UAE Air Force, 12 Mk.64s for Kuwait, 30 Mk.65s for Saudi Arabia, and 20 Mk.66s for Switzerland.

RIGHT: *The British Aerospace Hawk 100 is a development of the Hawk T.1, which was originally designed as an advanced trainer for the RAF. BAe decided that there was a market for a moderately priced trainer/ fighter with sophisticated avionics and a substantial weapon carrying capability. With this in mind, it developed the Hawk 100 and single-seat 200 series. Fitted with a new wing, the airframe has undergone numerous validation flights with a wide permutation of fuel and weapons loads. These range from 60 per cent internal fuel and 3,000lb warload, permitting the full load factor of 8G to be attained, to four 1,000lb bombs and the gun pod, leaving a performance still capable of over 500kts.*

A further development of the Hawk is the T-45A Goshawk for the US Navy, which has been ordered from BAe and McDonnell Douglas. A total requirement of 300 is already in production and initial deliveries have commenced.

Export orders for the Hawk 100 and 200 series are for the Saudi Al Yamamah II programme, which may require a total of 60 but is yet to be confirmed, while Malaysia has ordered 10 Hawk 100 and 18 200s. The UAE Air Force has ordered 22 100s and 12 200s, funded by member Gulf states. Brunei is planning to purchase 16 Hawk 100s but this order has yet to be confirmed.

LEFT: *Part of the RAF Harrier force is allocated to the NATO reaction force – the Air Mobile Force (AMF) – and is employed on exercises to the northern and southern flanks. The Harrier T.4 and GR.3A formate on the wing of a VC.10 tanker after air-to-air refuelling. The Harriers have been given a temporary winter camouflage for operations in Norway. Due to the easing of tension between East and West, the exercises to these areas are to become less frequent.*

In 1982 Harrier GR.3s were deployed to the South Atlantic to provide a strike capability for the Task Force. They joined the Royal Navy Sea Harriers which were already deployed on the carriers. Although operating in the strike role, it was normal for the Harriers to fly with the Sidewinder AAM as well as their bomb load.

RIGHT: *The British Aerospace/ McDonnell Douglas Harrier II is shown here with a wide range of missiles it can carry to meet some of its roles. Visible on the ground at the extremes are the Active Skyflash AAM, inboard are a pair of Alarm anti-radar missiles, then a pair of ASRAAM – the next generation short range AAM and Sea Eagle anti-shipping missile. On the Harriers pylons are six AMRAAM medium-range AAM plus a pair of Sidewinder missiles.*

LEFT: *The RAF has been replacing its Harrier GR.3s with the GR.5. This is a larger aircraft developed with McDonnell Douglas from the AV-8B, currently in service with the USMC. It has the capability of carrying a far greater war load, for which it has seven under-wing and fuselage pylons, plus two additional pylons for the Sidewinder AAMs. It is also fitted with a pair of Aden 25mm cannon.*

The first GR.5 flew on 30th April 1985. The late deliveries are being fitted with a Forward Looking Infra-red (FLIR) system plus a Smiths Industries Head Up/Head Down display and cockpit displays compatible with Night Vision Goggles (NVG). Designated Harrier GR.7, these new fits will give the aircraft the capability of flying low-altitude attack missions by night as well as day and in adverse weather conditions. Eventually the GR.5s already delivered will be brought up to GR.7 standard.

A further order has also been placed for 14 of the Harrier T.10 two-seat trainers.

LEFT: *The Royal Navy Sea Harrier FRS.1 is commencing a mid-life update programme which will significantly increase the capability of the aircraft as well as changing its outward appearance. Designated Sea Harrier FRS.2, it is being fitted with the Ferranti Blue Vixen multi-mode pulse doppler radar. This will be the first European combat aircraft to be equipped with the Advanced Medium Range Air to Air Missile (AMRAAM). It will also have the capability of engaging multiple targets simultaneously beyond visual range. The first Sea Harrier FRS.2 will enter service with the Royal Navy in 1992.*

BELOW: *The AIM-9 Sidewinder has become the standard air-to-air missile (AAM) amongst the Western nations. Originally developed back in the early '50s by the US Naval Weapons Centre at China Lake, the first launch was on 11th September 1953 as the XAAM-N-7. The Sidewinder is a simple and cheap missile and as a result has been built in large numbers. Over 95,000 of the original AIM-9B were built in the US and Europe. Technological developments have seen a variety of improvements over the years, with many 9Bs being rebuilt, resulting in well over 26,000 AAMs of various marks being delivered. The guidance system was based on the detecting of an infra-red (IR) source. The missile locking on to this source would give the pilot an audible signal and the missile would be launched and follow the IR source until its hit was close, when the proximity fuse would trigger the warhead. In good conditions the missile was successful, but performance deteriorated in poor weather. It was also likely to become distracted by the sun or the reflection from a lake. The missile also needed to be launched from behind the target to detect the IR source.*

In 1977 the first of the AIM-9Ls appeared off the US production line, which represented a new generation with a major leap forward in the seeker head design. This gives the Sidewinder an all-aspect capability, and together with a revised warhead made this a highly potent weapon. Production of the AIM-9L has continued in the US as well as from a European consortium.

Development of the AIM-9 Sidewinder continues, with improvements to low-level capabilities and resistance to counter measures.

This pair of AIM-9Ls is fitted onto the pylon of a Royal Navy Sea Harrier FGR.1.

ABOVE: *The British Aerospace Sea Harrier FRS.1 first flew on 20th August 1978. Although based on the RAF Harrier, the Sea Harrier has a new forward fuselage, giving the pilot better all-round vision from the higher cockpit. It is fitted with the Blue Fox multi-mode radar, which will assist the pilot especially in the fighter role. A pair of two-seat Hunter airframes have been modified and fitted with the Blue Fox Radar and are used as trainers for the Sea Harriers. They have been designated T.8M. The Hunter from 899 Sqn has an inert training Sidewinder while the Sea Harrier has the AIM.9L.*

RIGHT: *The Sea Harrier FRS.1 is normally armed with two AIM-9L Sidewinder AAMs for its fighter role, although pylons were built during the Falklands conflict enabling four missiles to be carried.*

RIGHT: *The SEPECAT Jaguar was the result of Anglo-French collaboration during the '60s. It was designed as a supersonic light strike aircraft and the prototype first flew on 8th September 1968. A total of 202 were delivered to the RAF, which included 37 trainers designated T.2, the strike version being the GR.1. The RAF Jaguar equips two strike squadrons (6 and 54 Sqn (latter illustrated)), one reconnaissance (41 Sqn) and a training unit (226 OCU).*

RIGHT: *The Jaguar GR.1 flew a large number of sorties during the Gulf War and proved that, despite age, it was still an effective weapon. In addition to painting the aircraft pink, a shadow cockpit was painted underneath the fuselage to confuse the enemy. Markings have also been painted beneath the cockpit to indicate the number of sorties this particular aircraft flew during the war.*

LEFT: *The events in the Middle East during August 1990 led to the deployment of No. 6 (Composite) Squadron, equipped with Jaguar GR.1As, on the 11th August to the Gulf. The Squadron was made up from the three RAF Coltishall-based squadrons and flew direct to Cyprus assisted by Victor tankers. After a 24-hour stop-over, the Jaguars completed the flight to Thumrait in Oman, this time assisted with refuelling by the VC.10s of 101 Sqn.*

A number of additional ECM pods and other items of equipment were fitted, and the normal grey-green camouflage was covered in a more appropriate pink prior to their departure. The Jaguar is part of NATO's quick reaction team and thus used to having to move at short notice. Once in theatre the build-up period was put to good use, with numerous training sorties for an environment that was new to many of the Jaguar pilots.

RIGHT: *The RAF Jaguars carried personalised artwork during the deployment to the Gulf. While some were reminders of loved ones, real or imagined, others reflected the work to be done.*

LEFT: *The largest operator of the Jaguar within the RAF is 226 OCU, which is based at RAF Lossiemouth in Scotland. Besides converting aircrews from the Hawk to the Jaguar, 226 OCU pilots are taught the vital job of flying a fast jet at low level, as well as live weapon handling on the ranges.*

LEFT: *When Operation Granby/ Desert Storm drew to a halt on 3rd March 1991, Saddam Hussain remained in command in Iraq. Although his military power was severely weakened, he quickly worked on his own people to re-impose his authority. Much to the world's dismay, it was quickly discovered that his troops were firing on the Iraqi Kurds to the north and the Shi'ites to the south. In a short time refugees poured across the borders into Turkey and Iran, which were unable to cope with the numbers, so a military force returned to Iraq to protect the Kurds and help with food supplies.*

Currently the ground force has been withdrawn, but the situation is constantly monitored by recce Jaguars making a number of daily flights over Iraq from a base at Incirlik in Turkey. A multi-national reaction force remains in Turkey as a deterrent to the Iraqi military threat.

RIGHT: *Until recently the RAF Jaguar GR.1 and T.2 have only been fitted with a pair of 30mm Aden cannon which could be used for defensive armament. Tactics would rely on fighter cover and the Jaguars would try to avoid direct contact. The four pylons fitted under the wings, plus another under the fuselage, are normally used for long-range fuel tanks or up to a 10,000lb combination of fuel and weapons – usually bombs. During the Gulf War, depending on the mission, a fuel tank would be fitted under each wing for reconnaissance sorties. These were usually flown as pairs, with one aircraft fitted with the Vinten recce pod and the other with the BAe pod which included the F126 camera under the fuselage. Alternatively, a single fuel tank was fitted under the fuselage and bombs were fitted onto the inner pylons. Electronic defence pods were fitted on the outer wing pylons.*

RAF Jaguars were also equipped with over-wing missile pylons. These were introduced originally for the export Jaguar International. They provided self protection for the Jaguars with the fitting of the pair of Sidewinder missiles. This particular aircraft is fitted with the inert training missile.

LEFT: *The Indian Air Force initially received 18 ex-RAF Jaguar airframes as an interim measure. These were subsequently replaced by 40 new aircraft built by British Aerospace. At the same time plans were made for HAL to commence production in India. A total of 60 Jaguars were assembled in India from components supplied from BAe, and an increasing proportion was constructed by HAL.*

The Jaguar IS is from 14 Squadron and is armed with a pair of Magic AAMs.

RIGHT: *The French partners for BAC were Dassault, who built some 160 single- and 40 two-seat aircraft for the French Air Force, plus a naval prototype.*

The Jaguar has only seen moderate export success. Besides sales to Ecuador (12), Oman (25) and Nigeria (18), the Indian Air Force is the largest overseas operator of the Jaguar, with over 100 in service. The Matra Magic AAM was built by France in direct competition to the Sidewinder and has an interchangeable capability. An inert training round of the Matra R.550 Magic AAM missile can be seen being loaded on to the overwing pylon of an Indian Air Force Jaguar.

RIGHT: *The Tornado GR.1 is the RAF's main strike aircraft. The result of collaboration with Germany and Italy, the first prototype made its maiden flight on 14th August 1974. A total of 219 GR.1s were ordered for the RAF, but one batch of 33 was subsequently cancelled in 1990 as part of the defence cuts resulting from the breaking down of the East/West confrontation.*

The Tornado entered RAF service in 1980 with the Tri-national Tornado Training Establishment at RAF Cottesmore. From here all NATO Tornado crews receive their type training before progressing on to weapons training. The Tornado GR.1 was ordered as a replacement for the Canberra and Vulcan bombers, and will soon replace the Buccaneers. It is a capable strike aircraft able to carry some 18 tonnes of weapons on pylons under the wing and fuselage.

This Tornado GR.1 is from 29 Sqn.

LEFT: *The RAF Tornado GR.1s saw much action during the Gulf war, and number of aircraft were lost during low-level attacks against Iraqi airfields using JP233. Once the job of disabling Iraqi airfields was done, higher-level attacks could be achieved without opposition and the losses dropped.*

Although fighter cover was provided for the strike missions, in common with most other strike aircraft, the Tornado GR.1s were fitted with a pair of Sidewinder AAMs, one of which can be seen on the rail attached to the underwing fuel tank pylon. A quantity of the improved AIM-9Ms were obtained from the US to replace the AIM-9Ls normally carried.

RIGHT: *A variant of the Tornado GR.1 has been adapted for the reconnaissance role and is designated the GR.1a. It is fitted with an imaging system comprising of the Vinten 4000 horizon-to-horizon infra-red linescan, plus side-facing infra-red sensors forward of the air intakes. All the images are recorded on six video recorders – no photographic film is used. A total of six Tornado GR.1As were deployed to the Gulf, where they flew 128 operational sorties and clocked up some 300 hours. All sorties were flown at night, usually at 200ft and at speeds in excess of 500kts.*

The RAF has two reconnaissance squadrons equipped with the Tornado GR.1a: 2 Squadron (illustrated) and 13 Squadron.

ABOVE: *The Italians are the third partners in the Tornado programme and they ordered 99 for their Air Force. All the Italian AF Tornados are the IDS attack version, with one squadron to be equipped with HARM. An order was placed for 16 ECR Tornados but these were cancelled as part of the 1991 defence budget cuts. A project has restarted to modify an existing IDS airframe as a cheaper solution.*

Eight aircraft from 1540 Stormo/ 60 Gruppo and 1560 Stormo/360 Gruppo were deployed and saw action in the Gulf War on Operation

Locusta as part of the Allied Force.

The Tornado is flying at speed with the wings fully swept. An additional pod can be seen under the fuselage which enables it to act as a buddy-to-buddy tanker. This method would normally be used when the aircraft is on a deep penetration sortie which would require extra fuel but which is not practical for an accompanying large tanker. While the RAF has a substantial tanker force the German Air Force has no dedicated tankers. The Italians are modifying four Boeing 707s for this role.

ABOVE: *In 1985 the Saudi Government placed an order, known as Al Yamamah, for a defence package with British Aerospace which included 48 Tornado GR.1s. A number of these saw action with the RSAF during the Gulf War. Six of these Tornados are being delivered as the reconnaissance variant – similar to the RAF GR.1A.*

Although not yet signed, Al Yamamah II is likely to require a further quantity, possibly doubling the original order.

LEFT: *The Germans are a partner of Panavia who manage the Tornado programme. Of the strike variant, 212 were ordered for the German Air Force. Deliveries commenced in 1982, replacing the Starfighter in the strike role. An order for 35 of an ECR variant has also been delivered.*

ROYAL SAUDI AIR FORCE القوات الجوية الملكية السعودية

MARINE

43+68

LEFT: *In addition to the Tornado equipping the German Air Force, 112 examples were ordered for the German Navy. As with the German Air Force, the Navy Tornados were ordered to replace the Starfighter used in the maritime role. Tasks include reconnaissance and strike missions against shipping. For the latter it is equipped with the Kormoran missile.*

Deliveries were initially MFG.1 (illustrated), followed by MFG.2.

ABOVE: *One of the requirements of a capable fighter is that it must have the ability to intercept at an effective distance from the potential target. The predecessor to the Tornado – the Lightning – was very effective in being able to intercept a possible target quickly. However, in its early days this was where its problem started, as it also very quickly burnt its fuel: on full afterburner it could burn all its fuel in six minutes. The solution was to refuel the Lightning in flight. Initially this was done from converted Valiant bombers and then later from the converted Victor. The Lightning, being a gas guzzler, tended to be a reactionary fighter, at which it was very effective. Its Combat Air Patrol (CAP) capability was always heavily reliant on air-to-air refuelling. The Phantom later* joined the Lightning in the air defence role and was better on CAP, with its drop tanks giving extra fuel capacity.

The Tornado changed the whole concept. One of its main advantages was that it was fitted with fuel efficient turbofan engines. The variable geometry (vg) wing means that it is able to loiter in the patrol area with wings forward and at an economical speed. When a potential target is tracked the Tornado converts to a high-speed fighter by sweeping the wings back. This vg configuration can give a loiter of two hours without refuelling, on top of the transit; when refuelled this could be extended many times.

RIGHT: *The Tornado variable geometry wings can be set at 25°, which extends the lower end of its speed range. This enables a reasonable approach speed which, together with its reverse thrust, gives a very short landing run. At the other extreme the wings can be swept back to 67° for high-speed flight. The on-board computer automatically selects the correct wing angle according to the speed. Here the wings are swept forward.*

LEFT: *To protect the Tornado and most front line strike and fighter types a NATO programme of construction of Hardened Aircraft Shelters (HAS) is now virtually complete. Capable of housing one or two Tornados, the HAS is built of specially strengthened concrete to give the aircraft good protection in the event of an attack. The HAS is so designed that during an alert period the aircraft can be fuelled, armed and started while still in the HAS, the doors only being opened when the aircraft is ready for take off, thus leaving the aircraft vulnerable for the minimum time. Likewise, as soon as the aircraft lands, it taxis straight to the HAS and is winched in backwards and the doors shut. The aircraft can be turned round in relative safety.*

INSERT ABOVE: *In addition to a strike aircraft the RAF required a fighter to replace the Lightning and Phantom. The solution was the Air Defence Variant (ADV), of which a total of 165 were ordered. Initial deliveries were to the F.2 standard, but these were soon superseded by the improved F.3, with the original batch to be upgraded.*

RIGHT: *An RAF Tornado F.3 makes a high-speed pass during a training sortie. It is basically a clean airframe, with wings fully swept and no missiles or under-wing fuel tanks fitted. The rails for the Sidewinder missiles can be clearly seen under the wings as can the recesses under the fuselage to accommodate the Skyflash missiles.*

RIGHT: *A pair of Tornado F.3s of No. 111 Sqn based at RAF Leuchars in Scotland on patrol over the North Sea. Until 1970 the Tornado fighters had to rely on ground radar or the Shackleton AEW.2 to provide radar coverage. The entry into service of the Boeing Sentry AEW.1 has improved coverage dramatically, and resulted in a far more effective air defence force.*

RIGHT: *The Tornado F.3 equips two squadrons of the Royal Saudi Air Force, Nos 29 and 34 Squadrons, which were ordered from British Aerospace as part of the Al Yamamah defence package. To reduce the effect of the extreme heat in the region, the cockpit canopy is covered.*

RIGHT: *This Tornado F.3 is from the RAF No. 5 Squadron based at RAF Leeming. Having been warned by Norwegian radar of the tracking of an unknown aircraft radar return approaching the top of its region, RAF Strike Command scrambles a Tornado to investigate. The aircraft turns out to be a Soviet Tupolev Tu-95, codenamed "Bear" by NATO. Flying in international airspace the "Bear" had as much right to be flying in the area as the Tornado. In the past the "Bears" would frequently fly towards UK airspace to test the defence reaction. The current variants are now usually the reconnaissance version, known as a "Bear D", and it would be intercepted and escorted away from the UK Air Defence Region (UKADR).*

The RAF fighters have become more effective with air-to-air refuelling and the interceptions would happen further out over the North Sea, until now they are achieved not far off the Norwegian coast. A tanker is also scrambled and the escort can be maintained with air-to-air refuelling for as long as necessary. With the reduction of the East/West tension it is thought that these intercepts will become a token gesture.

LEFT: *An RAF Tornado F.3 on CAP in the Gulf makes an interesting comparison to the Tornado F.3 on the bottom of page 31. This aircraft has its full complement of four Skyflash radar-guided AAMs and four AIM-9M Sidewinder infra-red-seeking AAMs. It is also fitted with a pair of under-wing fuel tanks to enable it to remain on station for longer periods. A number of upgrades were made to virtually all of the aircraft which were to be operated in the Gulf to enhance their capabilities. To the rear of the Sky Flash missiles can be seen one of these in the form of packs of flares which would be fired to distract any heat seeking missile launched at them by the Iraqis.*

LEFT: *A Tornado F.3 of No. 11 (Composite) Squadron at RAF Leeming on 22nd September 1990. All the Tornados deployed from the UK had been subject to numerous modifications to enhance their capabilities and survivability. Only those deployed straight from APC in Cyprus were unmodified. The crew climb aboard ready for the long ferry flight out to the Gulf, where they assisted in providing the CAP for the Allied forces. The large flaps on top of the fuselage, either side of the tail, are air brakes.*

RIGHT: *The intrepid aircrews taxi out with their fully-armed Tornado F.3s to a hostile environment for an unknown period and an unknown future. The joined a mixed but impressive Allied fighter force which included F-14s, F-15s, F-18s and Mirage 2000s.*

ABOVE: *This could be a taste of the future fighter for Europe. The European Aircraft Programme (EAP) was the proof of concept aircraft for the next generation of fighter for NATO – the EFA. It was an international programme initially co-produced by aircraft manufacturers in the UK, Germany and Italy, and later including Spain.*

Germany has now announced its probable withdrawal from the project.

RIGHT: *The European Fighter Aircraft (EFA) is a £21-billion project combining the future fighter requirements of Britain, Germany, Italy and Spain. In RAF service it will replace the Jaguar and Phantom and later the Tornado F.3. A planned requirement of 250 exists and an eventual development into a ground attack model may increase its*

demand. Germany originally required a similar quantity but following Reunification this has been cancelled. Italy has also reduced her requirement from 160 to 130 to replace the F-104S Starfighter. Spain has likewise reduced her requirement from 100 to 87.

ABOVE: *The EAP first took to the air on the 8th August 1986 and has been the subject of numerous trials and tests. It has been flown fitted with Skyflash and ASRAAM AAMs.*

The ASRAAM (Advanced Short Range Air to Air Missile) is a British requirement for a missile to replace the AIM-9L/M Sidewinder for the RAF EFA and Harrier as well as the RN Sea Harrier. It is a fire-and-forget missile, which the pilot can launch at one enemy aircraft up to 10 kilometres range and then engage another aircraft while the first missile is still homing in on its target. The ASRAAM has been subject to a lengthy development for NATO fighters. In 1988 BAe took over the project, which faltered when the Germans decided to withdraw. In March 1991 the British Government placed a £570 million order with BAe for the development and manufacture of the missile. This was in competition with the French MICASRAAM and a further upgrade of the Sidewinder.

ABOVE: *The AMX was originally designed for the Italian Air Force as a single-seat combat aircraft capable of ground attack, reconnaissance and some fighter roles. The AMX first flew on the 15th May 1984. The Italian Air Force plan that five attack/reconnaissance groups will be equipped with 187 of the single-seat aircraft, ordered to replace the G-91 and F-104G Starfighter. At least 51 two-seat trainers will also be delivered.*

RIGHT: *The AMX is the result of a collaborative project between Aeritalia of Italy and Embraer of Brazil. Both countries had identified a requirement for a light strike aircraft.*

This example is the Brazilian Air Force single-seat version, of which 79 are on order. An additional 15 two-seat trainers are also on order. Both can be fitted with the AIM-9 Sidewinder AAM.

LEFT: *The PZL130 Turbo Orlik is a two-seat primary, basic and multi-purpose training aircraft. It is the development of the civilian aircraft which first flew on the 13th July 1986. It is being designed for the Polish Air Force as a flying simulator with a cockpit which resembles that of the Sukhoi Su-22. It is powered by the Motorlet Walter M601 turboprop and has six underwing pylons. Although primarily a trainer, the Turbo Orlik has a secondary combat role of anti-helicopter attack.*

ABOVE: *The Spanish-built CASA C-101 was designed to meet a Spanish Air Force requirement for a training aircraft and took to the air for the first time on the 27th June 1977. Manufacturers of most current training aircraft have included some weapons training capability. Thus, with minimal adaption the aircraft is capable of carrying out a variety of roles. While these other tasks may not be carried out to the optimum ability, the small cost in converting the trainer to a strike aircraft or fighter makes this type of force cost-effective and attractive. As can be seen with this weapon display, the CASA C-101 has the capability of carrying a wide range of weapons for bombing, strafing, anti-shipping or fighter, for which a pair of the Matra R.550 Magic missiles can be fitted.*

In addition to the 88 delivered to the Spanish Air Force, deliveries have been made to Chile, Honduras and Jordan.

LEFT: *The Fiat G-91 was the result of a NATO requirement for a light fighter/strike aircraft. It first flew on 9th August 1956, but despite the fact that it was proposed as the standard NATO aircraft for the role, it was only built by Italy and Germany under licence for their respective air forces. As a light fighter the current G-91 is equipped with a pair of 30mm DEFA 552 cannon plus four underwing pylons onto which a variety of AAMs can be fitted.*

Over the years the G-91 has been adapted to include armed reconnaissance, for which the nose was modified to include cameras. The next variant to appear was the two-seat trainer G-91T, achieved with a stretched fuselage. This was followed by a twin-engined development with a 60 per cent increase in power and designated G-91Y, which served only with the Italian AF.

The German G-91s have been withdrawn and a number were supplied to the Portuguese Air Force. This particular example belongs to 301 Squadron. All NATO squadrons with a tiger in their badge gather for the annual "Tiger Meet", and over the years the markings have become progressively more elaborate.

ABOVE: *The F-104 Starfighter was Lockheed's answer to the requirement for a high performance fighter. Conceived at a time when the Sabre was the fastest aircraft flying, the Starfighter was proposed at the outset to have a maximum speed of Mach 2.2. The final design was basically a jet engine with a pilot and stub wings. The wings were extremely thin – only four inches at the thickest point – and with a leading edge so sharp that a protective cover was required when on the ground for crew safety. It first flew on 4th March 1954 and entered service with the USAF in 1958 but suffered a troubled existence.*

In 1959 a controversial international programme came into being whereby the Belgian, Canadian, Danish, Dutch, German, Italian, Norwegian as well as the Japanese Governments decided that the Starfighter would become their new multi-mission attack fighter. The F-104G, as it became known, now had a better chance of becoming an outstanding fighter with an impressive speed capability and was fitted with an effective fire control radar. The Germans were the largest users of the Starfighter with nearly 1,000 ordered but they soon became concerned with the high loss rate. Over the years their air and ground crews became better experienced, but the Starfighter retained its bad name.

Despite these problems the Starfighter has been operated by many countries, including those listed above, plus Greece, Jordan, Pakistan, Taiwan (illustrated) and Turkey.

The Starfighter has been withdrawn from many of its original operators, although a number have been passed on to other air forces.

BELOW: *The Italian Air Force is another large user of the Starfighter. Initial deliveries were of the F-104Gs, but these have been replaced by over 200 of the Aeritalia-built F-104S. This particular aircraft is from 21 Squadron which is another of NATO's Tiger Squadrons and which was appropriately marked for the meet at the IAT '91. A Czech Mig-29 was an honorary guest and can be seen in the background.*

LEFT: *The Northrop F-5A/B Freedom Fighter was the successful bidder for the US Government's requirement for a suitable, relatively inexpensive, lightweight, high-performance fighter to be supplied under the Military Assistance Programme (MAP). First flown on 30th July 1959 as the private venture N-156C, it was not approved until 1962, and the actual prototype F-5 made its maiden flight in 1963. During this period the USN and USAF became interested in the supersonic trainer proposal, which was based on this design and which became the T-38 Talon.*

As a fighter the F-5 was armed with two nose-mounted Colt-Browning 20mm guns plus an AIM-9 Sidewinder fitted on each wingtip. As a strike aircraft nearly three tons of weapons could be carried on the five pylons.

The F-5 was widely used, and this example is from the Royal Netherlands Air Force, which took delivery of a total of 105 Canadair-built CF-5A/5Ds. It is painted in the markings of the Double Dutch display team, to celebrate the 75th Anniversary of the Royal Netherlands Air Force.

LEFT: *The Royal Jordanian Air Force ordered 44 F-5E plus two F-5Fs from the US in 1972 as part of its major re-equipment programme. In addition it took delivery of 30 surplus F-5As and four F-5Bs from Iran.*

This pair, in an appropriate desert camouflage, are F-5Es from No. 9 Squadron based at the Jordanian airfield, H-5. They are fitted with Sidewinder AAMs.

RIGHT: *While Northrop built nearly 900 F-5A/B and RF-5s variants, production was also undertaken in Spain by CASA, and by Canadair in Canada. A total of 240 F-5s were built by Canadair, of which 89 CF-5As and 46 CF-5Ds were delivered to the CAF. These equated to the Northrop F-5A single-seat fighters and F-5B two-seat trainers. They entered service in 1968. A number of these aircraft are receiving upgrades which will greatly extend their lives. Although no longer being used as a front-line fighter, the CF-5 is considered a relatively inexpensive advanced trainer for fighter pilots progressing to the CF-18 Hornet.*

This Canadian Armed Forces CF-5A is from 419 Squadron and can be seen refuelling from a CC-137 tanker.

LEFT: While deliveries of the F-5A and two-seat F-5B were progressing, Northrop developed a substantially improved version by replacing the GE J85-GE-13s with J85-GE-21s. This gave an increase thrust of some 23 per cent which, together with numerous modifications to improve the handling, resulted in the new variant being given a new name and designated the F-5E Tiger II. A two-seat version designated F-5F was also built which retained all the capabilities of the F-5E. Later, a reconnaissance version was produced and designated RF-5E.

The US military were sufficiently impressed with the F-5E that a number were purchased for use by the Navy's Fighter Weapon School and the Air Force's Aggressor Squadrons, where they are flown against current front-line fighters to represent potential enemy aircraft.

Illustrated is an F-5E Tiger II of the 527th TFS, which was based at RAF Alconbury and used to fly "against" most NATO fighter squadrons.

RIGHT: The Chilean Air Force took delivery of 15 F-5Es and 3 F-5Fs in 1974, following an embargo by the UK on further Hunter spares due to the Chileans poor record on human rights. Subsequently, spares for these, too, became the subject of a US arms embargo, but recent improvements have now led to a resumption of supply.

The red bands on the tail and wings are to indicate that, for exercise purposes, this represents an enemy aircraft .

BELOW: The Swiss Air Force purchased 98 F-5E Tiger IIs to replace the de Havilland Venoms which had been operated since the 1950s. They also took delivery of 12 F-5F trainers to replace the Vampires.

ABOVE: *Taiwan is a major operator of the F-5, with over 300 built at its Aero Industry Development Centre following a licence production agreement. Many of the F-5 of all variants are being upgraded to a greater or lesser degree with modifications being made to airframes, with additions to avionics.*

Nose up with the nose wheel OLEO extended, this F-5E is operated by No. 23 "Tsi chiang" Squadron of the Republic of China Air Force. This Squadron forms part of No. 4 Tactical Fighter Wing and is based at Chiayi Air Base in Taiwan. The nose oleo is extended to increase the angle of attack, thereby reducing the take-off and landing run.

ABOVE: *The Republic of Singapore Air Force (RoSAF) took delivery of over 40 of the F-5E/Fs between 1976 and 1989 for the fighter and attack roles. It is planned that eight of the F-5Es will be converted to the RF-5E configuration to provide a reconnaissance capability.*

This F-5E is from No. 144 Sqn which is based at Tangah Air Base. It operates the aircraft in two contrasting colour schemes for the air defence and training roles.

RIGHT: *This RoSAF F-5E sports a multi-tone grey camouflage. It is also from a late batch which has a few differences, a noticeable example of which is the additional fin fillet.*

LEFT: *The Indonesian Armed Forces (TNI-AU) operates 11 of the single-seat F-5Es together with four F-5F trainers. Currently they are flown operationally by 14 Squadron in the fighter role. It is probable that this may include the attack role following the introduction of the F-16.*

BELOW: *The Royal Malaysian Air Force received 14 F-5Es and F-5Bs in 1978 for No. 11 and 12 Squadrons based at Butterworth, which replaced the F-86 Sabre. Subsequently, the F-5Bs were passed to Thailand and additional Tiger IIs were obtained, which included F-5F trainers and the reconnaissance RF-5E.*

The nearest is the F-5E with a reconnaissance RF-5E in the middle, both from No. 11 Squadron. Leading the formation is a F-5F from No. 12 Squadron.

ABOVE: *The McDonnell F-15 evolved to meet the threat imposed by the Soviet MiG-25, which had proved itself capable of flying high-speed reconnaissance missions with impunity. Following a design competition construction commenced on the first F-15 and the prototype flew its maiden flight on 27th July 1972. The F-15 is a system-designed aircraft, in that the pilot has an extensive range of electronic aids and sensors to assist him. These have been designed to be included from outset and are housed inside the aircraft rather than being added on later in pods.*

Tactical Air Command (TAC) received its first F-15 when delivery was made to 1st TFW at Langley AFB on 9th January 1976. Such was the perceived threat that within two years, three squadrons of F-15s were deployed to Europe to match Soviet and East German aircraft.

The two F-15 illustrated are from the 32 TFS based at Soesterberg in Holland. They are seen here in their training fit with one Sidewinder AAM.

LEFT: *The F-15 was heavily utilised by the USAF and RSAF during the Gulf War to provide fighter cover for Allied forces. As a result the F-15s saw considerable action, especially during the early days of the war when Iraqi AF fighters were scrambled to intercept the Allied attack aircraft. It didn't take long for the Iraqis to realise that they were completely outclassed.*

The Iraqi AF fighter force included the very capable MiG-29 and Mirage F.1, but the initial Allied strikes had damaged much of their ground-based radar and control centres. This left the fighters to rely on their own radar to track and attack hostile incoming aircraft. The Allied forces were so well equipped that each attacking wave of aircraft included anti-radar HARM or Alarm missiles which would attack any ground based radar still operating, as soon as it was switched on.

The Iraqi fighters were radar equipped, but this had limited range and they would instantly give their position away and were likely to be quickly attacked. At the same time the Allied fighters were provided with radar cover from the Boeing E.3 "AWACS" flying radar station, which was flown at a safe distance and gave vectors to intercept Iraqi aircraft without giving the fighter position away. As a result the F-15s destroyed 36 of the 41 Iraqi aircraft/helicopters lost in combat. This particular aircraft was credited with two "kills".

RIGHT: *A McDonnell F-15C Eagle from 36 TFW based at Bitburg in Germany has flames spouting from its afterburners as it roars up to the blue after receiving the signal to scramble. It is powered by a pair of P&W F100 turbofans which each develop 14,500lbs of thrust. By injecting neat fuel into the exhaust this thrust can be boosted to 24,000lbs. While rapidly depleting the fuel carried, it can rocket the F-15 to 65,000ft.*

During the Gulf War, twelve USAF F-15Cs were transferred to the Royal Saudi Air Force from Bitburg, and a further 12 from Soesterberg in Holland, to boost the number already operated by the Saudis for air defence.

LEFT: *As part of an effective defence force, fighters are maintained at an alert status 24 hours a day, 365 days a year. When a return on a ground or airborne early warning radar cannot be identified, the fighters are scrambled to investigate. Often this can be a false alarm, with the offending aircraft having a radio or transponder failure. Occasionally the scramble is for real. In this case it is a Soviet Tu-95 "Bear" flying in international airspace to monitor the movements and signals of a NATO naval exercise. As such the "Bear" would be shadowed by fighter aircraft. On this occasion the "Bear" is being escorted by an RAF Tornado F.3 from 5 Squadron and an F-15C Eagle from 57 FIS based at Keflavik in Iceland. Both fighters can be armed with Sidewinder and Sparrow AAMs, although the F-15 only appears to have two Sparrows fitted.*

LEFT: *An F-15A from 36 TFW, based at Bitburg in Germany, positions on a KC-135 Stratotanker. The boom of the tanker has been lowered to indicate to the receiver that the tanker is available and that he is cleared to move into position at the rear of the tanker. Once in position the boom operator will manoeuvre the boom with a joystick controller which transfers the movements down to the "V" shape wings until the end is in line with the receiver's receptacle. In this case the receptacle is in the black area in the wing root of the F-15A, visible between the boom and the left control wing. When they are lined up the boom is further extended until the connection is made. Once locked in position the fuel transfer can commence.*

Whilst this is comparatively easy in good weather conditions it is a completely different matter in bad weather or at night. In peacetime, radio communications can be made so that the pilots may contact each other, but in time of war the actions have to be made in complete radio silence.

The first fighter to deploy to the Gulf were F-15Cs from the 27th and 71st TFS from Langley AFB. Through the use of in-flight refuelling provided by KC-135s and KC-10s, the aircraft were able to fly direct to Dhahran, a distance of 6,500 miles, on 7th August 1991.

LEFT: *Refuelling played a major feature during the Gulf War, with virtually every mission requiring tanking to complete. The refuelling capability is known as a force multiplier, as it enables the same number of tactical aircraft to achieve far greater results. A fighter, for instance, can only remain airborne for a limited period of time, and this is dependent on the rate at which it uses its fuel. To calculate the effective time on station the transit time must be deducted. With a tanker supplying fuel when required the fighter can remain on station as long as the pilot is capable.*

BELOW: *An F-15C from the 33 TFW, based at Eglin AFB, launches an AIM-7F Sparrow at a target. The Raytheon AIM-7 Sparrow is a radar guided, supersonic, all-weather, all-aspect AAM; that is it can be fired at an aircraft flying in any direction. It is also resistant to countermeasures. The Sparrow is fitted to USAF and USN F-4s, F-14s, F-15s, F-16s and A/F-18s.*

RIGHT: *A development of the F-15 fighter is the F-15E Strike Eagle. As its name implies, this variant of the F-15 has been designed to take full advantage of its fighter capabilities and combine them with a strike role, with pylons carrying bombs. It can also carry Sidewinder and Sparrow AAMs. Provision has also been made to carry the AIM-120, which is currently known as AMRAAM. In addition to its fighter avionics the F-15E is fitted with the LANTIRN system allowing low-level navigation, together with a laser designator which is able to illuminate the target up to 10 miles away. Rather than fitting long-range fuel tanks, slipper tanks have been developed which bolt onto the outside of the fuselage under the wings. This is aerodynamically more efficient than the underwing tanks, creating less drag as well as leaving the pylons clear to carry other stores. It is capable of carrying some 24,500lbs of external payload and, combined with the pair of P&W F100-PW-129 engines which develop over 58,000lb thrust, gives the F-15E an extremely useful performance.*

The 48th Tactical Fighter Wing, based at RAF Lakenheath in the UK, is the first USAFE unit to operate the F-15E Strike Eagle. It currently flies the F-111F which it operated successfully during the Gulf War. By the end of 1992 the Wing should have fully converted to the F-15E.

LEFT: *The role of a fighter is to provide protection for a potential target. Whilst this is frequently a ground location such as an airfield, it can also be another aircraft. An AEW aircraft will operate in a "safe" area but will have a protective screen near at hand, while strike aircraft, when it is considered necessary, will have fighter aircraft fly at least part of the mission with them. This B-52 Stratofortress is being escorted by a pair of F-15As from 318 FIS, based at McCord AFB.*

When production of the F-15C finished in 1989 a total of 409 of this variant had been built for the USAF. In addition, 365 F-15As, 59 F-15Bs and 61 F-15Ds had also been delivered.

The restructuring of the USAF will result in several composite wings for specific roles. One such wing will be created at Mountain Home AFB and will comprise the E-3A Sentry providing AEW, F-15C/D/E Eagles for fighter cover and strike, plus KC-10 and KC-135 tankers. Thus able to act as a complete rapid intervention force, they will be part of the new Air Mobility Command (AMC), which comprises the old Strategic Air Command (SAC) and Tactical Air Command (TAC).

RIGHT: *The F-16 was the winner of a competition for a new lightweight fighter for the USAF and USN back in 1972, the choice having been narrowed down between General Dynamics and Northrop. Each was given a contract to build two prototypes and the results were then test flown. During the trials it transpired that there was little to choose between the aircraft. However, the USAF opted for the F-16. Northrop didn't lose out with their design – known as the YF-17 – as it was modified and then adopted by the USN as the F-18 Hornet.*

Shortly after the USAF selected the F-16, a number of NATO countries (Belgium, Denmark, Netherlands and Norway) made the same choice, basically to replace their Starfighters. As with the Starfighter programme, the F-16s were also to be built in Europe.

The F-16 Fighting Falcon, as it was subsequently named, has a high degree of sophistication within the cockpit to provide the pilot with a maximum field of view and efficiency. The 30° angle of the seat and the position of the controls are vital for an aircraft which has the capability of sustaining 9g while maintaining reasonable comfort for the pilot during air-to-air combat.

The 50 TFW, based at Hahn in Germany, is equipped with the F-16C. Here, four of their aircraft formate on the recently re-engined KC-135R Stratotanker - recognisable by the larger GE/SNECMA F108 (CFM56) turbofan engines from the originally equipped KC-135A, which apart from being less powerful, were a lot noisier and less fuel efficient.

RIGHT: *General Dynamics designed the F-16 with a modular airframe to enable future concepts to be more easily accommodated. A number of designs have materialised in addition to the normal evolution. These include demonstration engine changes from the P&W F100 to the F101 and the GE J79.*

A Control Configured Vehicle (CCV) emerged in the mid '70s, fitted with a pair of inlet-mounted control surfaces. These enable the aircraft to be controlled in a different way from normal in that turns can be simply achieved without banking, which could provide a more accurate platform for weapon launching. A further development of this configuration evolved in 1982 with the AFTI/F16, in which the new laws learned with the CCV were applied

into mission profiles and advanced cockpit controls and displays, including voice control.

A further development emerging in 1892 was the F-16XL, a derivative of the F-16 with a distinctive, arrow-shaped wing which more than doubles its area. It also has a 56in longer fuselage, and together these measures provides an 82 per cent increase in fuel economy. Drag is also reduced by 53 per cent (for equivalent loadings). To the pilot this means a much higher performance which will enable him to fly either with double the payload or for twice the distance.

To date the F-16XL remains a prototype without any orders but, following the success of the F-16 in the Gulf, perhaps this may become another shape to look out for.

ABOVE: *A further role for the F-16 is that of the Wild Weasel, originally developed in Vietnam with the F-105. Equipped with anti-radar missiles, the role of the Wild Weasel aircraft is to accompany or precede strike aircraft on a mission. While en route, if any signals from enemy ground-based radar are detected, the Wild Weasel launches one of its anti-radiation missiles which homes in on the transmission source and destroys it. The radar's only defence is for it to be switched off, which will enable the strike aircraft to proceed undetected.*

The first F-16Cs were delivered to the USAF in 1984 and provided two additional capabilities: automatic terrain following for night or bad weather operations as well as an improved air-to-air capability against multiple targets.

This F-16C is fitted with an AGM-45 Shrike anti-radiation missile in addition to a training Sidewinder AAM. The sole European Wild Weasel unit is 52 TFW, which is based at Spangdahlem in Germany. As part of the policy of flexibility the current F-4G Phantoms will be replaced by a total of 18 A-10 and OV-10s plus 18 F-16C/Ds. However, with the success of the F-4G in the Gulf this may be reviewed.

LEFT: *The 113 TFW is an Air National Guard unit based at Andrews AFB, near Washington, and is equipped with the F-16A Fighting Falcon.*

The ANG provides over 25 per cent of the Air Force's tactical fighter assets. These include the F-4, A-7, A-10 and F-15 in addition to the F-16. The conversion of the last F-4D Phantom unit to F-16 marked the complete modernisation of the ANG air defence capability. With the deactivation of the last active duty Air Defence squadron, the ANG has now taken over sole responsibility for the air defence of the continental United States.

The F-16 is normally equipped with a pair of wing tip mounted AIM-9 Sidewinder AAMs. For the fighter role it would also be fitted

with a further four Sidewinders or a pair of the AIM-7 Sparrows. It is also fitted with a 20mm Vulcan gun.

During Desert Shield two ANG F-16 units were mobilised and deployed to the Gulf. The 138th TFS from Syracuse were based at Al Kharj in Saudi Arabia. From there they flew 1,411 combat sorties, during which they accumulated over 3,700 hours and dropped over three million pounds of ordnance. In addition the 157th TFS from McEntire ANGB were located in eastern Saudi Arabia. The 706th TFS of the Air Force Reserve (AFRes) was also mobilised.

In total, 249 F-16s were deployed to the Gulf. During their deployment they flew 13,000 sorties and maintained a 95.2 per cent mission capable rate.

LEFT: *The 53 Danish Air Force F-16As and 21 F-16Bs were also built at SABCA as part of the European production agreement. Visible alongside the engine exhaust nozzle are the split trailing edge airbrakes.*

LEFT: *Although the F-16 was designed as a light fighter it wasn't long before other roles for the aircraft were explored. It soon became apparent that it would make a very capable strike aircraft and could carry a useful weapons load.*

This early F-16A Fighting Falcon from 466 TFS carries a pair of 2,000lb Mk.84 low-profile bombs in addition to four Sidewinder AAMs and an ALQ-119/184 ECM Pod.

BELOW: *The USAF 35 TFS, 8 TFW, based at Kunsan Air Base, which is also in the Republic of Korea, operates this unusually camouflaged F-16C, which is appropriately dubbed the "Water Melon".*

LEFT: *An enhancement to the F-16 for the all-weather strike role has been the addition of the Low Altitude Navigation and Targeting Infra-red for Night (LANTIRN) pod, together with some advanced electronic warfare systems. The LANTIRN system enables the pilot to fly low-level, automatic terrain following missions at night or in poor weather conditions. To assist the pilot's night mission role and target acquisition, the standard head-up display is replaced by a screen on which the enhanced external picture is visible, together with the normal head-up display information.*

The F-16Cs of 51 TFW, based at Osan Air Base in the Republic of Korea, are the only LANTIRN-equipped Fighting Falcons in the Far East. On the wing of the nearest aircraft is a Maverick Air to Ground (AGM) TV guided missile in addition to the Sidewinder AAM.

ABOVE: Another European production line was set up in Belgium, at the SABCA factory in Gossellies. Here 96 F-16As and 20 F-16Bs were constructed for the Belgian Air Force. This particular aircraft has been specially painted to celebrate the 45th Anniversary of No. 349 Squadron, based at Beauvechain.

RIGHT: The Pakistan Air Force operates the Fighting Falcon with 34 F-16As delivered, plus at least 14 F-16Bs. Based at PAF Base Sargodha, this pair of F-16As from No. 11 Squadron are on patrol and armed with Sidewinders.

During the period 1979-89, when the Pakistan Air Force was trying to prevent Afghan and Soviet Air Force aircraft from violating its airspace, the F-16s were frequently scrambled. For those intruders flying less capable aircraft that did not turn back early enough, the intercept often ended with their destruction.

BELOW: The Republic of Korea Air Force is equipped with 30 F-16Cs and six F-16D two-seat training variants. This three-ship fighter formation from 161 TFS, 11 TFW, halt at the end of the runway at Taegu Air Base, their home, awaiting instructions to launch.

ABOVE: *Amongst the latest forces to take delivery of the Fighting Falcon is the Bahrain Amiri Air Force, who have ordered a total of 12 F-16C and D models, of which this is the latter. It is fitted with a pair of the AIM-9P Sidewinders, which have a new motor and fuse and an improved reliability over earlier models.*

LEFT: *The F-16 is fitted with movable flaps on the wings' leading and tailing edges, which are computer controlled to give the optimum configuration for lift in all aspects of flight according the speed of the aircraft. Further lift is generated by the strakes which extend from the neatly-fared wing roots forward to beneath the cockpit. In addition, the strakes improve directional stability and roll control as well as preventing wing-root stall and reducing buffeting.*

Flying clean, and with afterburner blazing, this F-15A Fighting Falcon is one of 60 purchased by the Norwegian Air Force. A further 12 F-16B trainers were also ordered. These aircraft were built under licence by Fokker at Schiphol together with 177 for the Royal Netherlands Air Force as part of the European programme.

RIGHT: *The term fighter, when applied to the General Dynamics F-111, is something of a misnomer in that at a maximum take-off weight of around 100,000lbs (nearly double that of the F-15) it is somewhat overweight for a fighter. Initially planned to become a strike aircraft to replace the F-105 for the USAF and an air defence fighter for the USN, the first flight of the prototype F-111A was on 21st December 1964. Intensive flight testing highlighted many problems, especially with the navy variant. This finally resulted in its cancellation four years later when it was decided that it was unable to meet the Navy performance specifications.*

The F-111A, developed for the USAF, initially fared only slightly better when the 428 TFS took six aircraft to Thailand for operational trials over Vietnam. In four weeks three of them had been lost.

In 1972/3, following modifications, a wing of 48 F-111As was deployed to Vietnam. These were far more successful, and only six aircraft were lost during over 4,000 combat missions.

An F-111A from 366 TFW, based at Mountain Home AFB, can be seen dropping 24 500lb low profile bombs.

LEFT: *The General Dynamics F-111E resulted from experience in operating the F-111As. A total of 94 of this variant were built and were issued to equip the 20th TFW based at RAF Upper Heyford in the UK.*

A number were used on the raid on Libya and they were used in strength with great effect during Desert Storm. This particular aircraft was credited with 18 Gulf missions. The F-111Es of 20 TFW will be returning to the USA as part of the US defence budget cuts.

RIGHT: *The Allied forces used a wide range of weaponry to achieve the destruction of the Iraqi military might. In addition to the conventional iron bombs a large quantity of hi-tech weaponry was used, including the laser-guided "smart" bombs (LGBs) carried by F-111s, Tornados and the F-117s.*

In the past Hardened Aircraft Shelters (HAS) were constructed all over NATO airfields to protect the front line aircraft. The protection provided by these defences must give some cause for concern as these massive HAS have all been destroyed with single LGB weaponry.

RIGHT: *The F-111F is the ultimate F-111 variant, but by the time it was developed it had become too expensive for the USAF to purchase in the quantities that it wished. As a result only 94 F-111F were purchased and used to equip the three squadrons which make up 48 TFW, based at RAF Lakenheath in the UK. The F-111F is powered by the TF30-P-100, which can give at least 5,000lbs more thrust than earlier F-111s. Its electronics are also much improved over earlier models and it is equipped with the Pave Tack laser-guided and GBU-15 data link weapons delivery systems.*

The Pave Tack can be seen under the fuselage of the F-111F. With this system the crew can acquire, track and designate ground targets by day or night for the delivery of laser, infrared and electro-optically guided weapons, providing surgical

accuracy. In addition to the Sidewinder missile, a pair of laser-guided GBU-15 bombs have been loaded under the wings.

Sixty-six F-111Fs from 48 TFW, which are based at RAF Lakenheath in the UK, were deployed to the Gulf. The F-111s were found to be highly successful for a variety of missions, which ranged from destroying bridges to dropping the GBU-28 4,700lb bombs on a 100ft deep underground command centre near Baghdad. They were credited with destroying 245 Hardened Aircraft Shelters (HAS) and were found to be highly effective in hitting armoured vehicles, of which they destroyed 920 with the combined use of the Laser Guided Bombs (LGBs) and the Pave Tack designator system.

The F-111Fs of 48 TFW are in the process of being exchanged for the F-15E Strike Eagle.

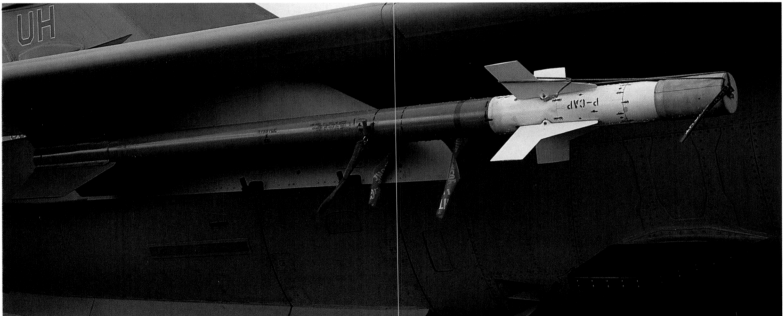

ABOVE: *As with the strike F-111s, the EF-111A Raven can be fitted with the Sidewinder AAM, primarily for self defence.*

RIGHT: *A number of F-111As have been modified for Electronic Warfare (EW) and re-designated the EF-111A Raven. As part of this modification the EF-111A has received similar electronic jamming equipment to that installed in the US Navy EA-6 Prowler.*

This EF-111A Raven of the 42 ECS is currently based at RAF Upper Heyford in England. A number of these aircraft were deployed to the Gulf and flew with strike missions, jamming Iraqi radar and radio communications.

BELOW: *The F-117A Stealth fighter has been the subject of speculation for many years. It was designed and built by Lockheed at the Skunk Works, which had previously produced the U-2 and SR-71A Blackbird and is famous for its revolutionary designs. The F-117A does not fall short in this department. Like the F-111 the Fighter designation is rather misleading, in that it more akin to a bomber, although it can carry air-to-air missiles.*

First flown on 18th June 1981, the F-117A remained an elusive mystery until it was first announced to the public in November 1988, five years after it entered service. Its existence was heavily publicised during the Gulf War, where the extreme accuracy of its weapon delivery, combined with a lack of radar signature, enabled the aircraft to operate effectively in a way no other could before.

These Lockheed F-117As are lined up at Langley AFB on 19th August 1991 ready for their deployment to the Gulf. These 20 aircraft were deployed by a squadron from the 37th TFW based at Tonopah.

RIGHT: *One of the F-117As deployed to the Gulf during Operation Desert Storm. This aircraft would appear to be a reversal of current thinking on aerodynamics. Gone are all the smooth curves to reduce drag, instead it is an aircraft comprising a number of flat surfaces which are so designed as to reflect radar energy away from the receiver. The F-117 is also coated in a black anti-radiation substance which, combined with the shape, make the aircraft almost completely invisible to radar. It is reputed that the biggest radar signature is from the pilots helmet. Because it is undetectable by radar the F-117 does not need speed as a defence, thus it has only a modest performance. Visible as a slot along the rear of the fuselage is the engine exhaust. This is so shaped as to spread the hot air and so reduce the infra-red signature.*

The F-117, referred to as shabba, or ghost, by the Saudis, comprised only 2.5 per cent of the USAF combat aircraft in Desert Storm. However, during the first 24 hours of the air campaign it was reputed to have struck 31 per cent of all targets. This was when the knocking out of Iraqi communications and other high value targets was the top priority.

RIGHT: *The F-117A, which looks as though its design comes from science fiction, takes on fuel from a KC-135 over the Gulf.*

The stealth characteristics mean that fewer aircraft are required to complete a mission. A standard mission of 32 attack aircraft with iron bombs would require 16 fighter escorts together with eight Wild Weasels for defence suppression and four radar jammers. This total force would require 15 tankers to refuel them all. To complete the same mission with F-117s would require only eight aircraft plus two tankers.

Due to the success of the F-117 during Desert Storm, provision was made in the 1992 US defence budget for re-opening the production line. It was thought likely that a further 12 aircraft were to be built to form a third squadron in addition to the 59 already in service, as suggested by the US Senate, but the proposal was dropped by Congress.

ABOVE: *The Fairchild A-10A Thunderbolt II is an aerial tank-buster and was first flown on 10th May 1972. Its main armament is the 30mm GAU-8/A Avenger Gatling gun fitted in the front fuselage. This can fire a depleted uranium round which can defeat most armour. The aircraft can also carry a wide range of weaponry on the eight underwing pylons, with an additional pair under the fuselage. It is powered by a pair of rear mounted GE TF34-GE-100 turbofans which generate 4,112kg of thrust each. Its maximum speed of 450kts may not be startling, but the A-10 is designed for manouverability, especially over the battlefield.*

The pilot is protected within a thick titanium box which can only be penetrated by heavy shells. All of the control systems are duplicated and separated to reduce the effect of any battle damage. Even the under-carriage is designed not to fully retract, so that if damage causes a hydraulic leak the aircraft can land with minimal damage.

The A-10A shown here is being refuelled from a KC-135 and is fitted with an ALE/ALQ-119 Electronic Counter Measures (ECM) pod under its left wing, while an AGM-65 Maverick TV-guided air-to-ground missile can be seen under its right wing.

RIGHT: *The Fairchild A-10A Thunderbolt II fires its GAU-8/A Avenger gatling gun, with a rate of 3,900 rounds per minute, at a ground target, while at the same time it ejects a flare to distract any heat-seeking missile that might be launched by the enemy ground forces.*

RIGHT: *After Desert Storm, the problems of the Iraqi Kurdish people erupted when Saddam Hussain decided that he would attack his own people with guns and tanks, as well as gunship helicopters, to restore complete control over his most productive regions. The Kurds in the north became refugees trying to escape from the attacks and pleaded with the rest of the world for help. With many thousands of starving Kurds in the mountains along the borders with Turkey and Iran, a series of air drops of food, tents and bedding was made by RAF and USAF Hercules over northern Iraq in Operation "Provide Comfort". Because of the threat of Iraqi ground fire, A-10s flew with the Hercules to provide cover. The markings on this aircraft indicate the number of sorties flown by this A-10A of the 81st TFW.*

LEFT: *An OA-10A Thunderbolt II from the USAFs 19 Tactical Air Support Squadron (TASS) based at Osan Air Base in South Korea. This variant replaces the Rockwell OV-10 Bronco as a mount for the Forward Air Controllers (FAC). As with the A-10, the OA-10 can carry the Sidewinder AAM for self defence.*

RIGHT: *Prior to the Gulf War the role of the A-10 in modern battle was in question, and there were rumours of it being withdrawn. It was slow and had no night or bad weather capability. Variants of the F-16 and A-7 were being considered as possible replacements.*

During Desert Shield 144 A-10s were deployed to the Gulf. Once Desert Storm commenced the A-10 came into its own to a devastating degree, proving its worth with large quantities of Iraqi equipment destroyed, as indicated by the "kill" tally on this particular aircraft. The ability of the A-10 to take punishment was also verified, with nearly half the deployed aircraft suffering some battle damage.

One particular A-10 was hit by what was thought to have been a hand-held SAM. This destroyed two of the three spars and removed over 20ft of skin from the upper wing surface. Despite an initial fire and loss of control, the pilot landed safely back at King Fahd Air Base. The Battle Damage Repair (BDR) team were able to have the aircraft back in the air four days later.*

The success of the A-10 "Warthog" means that it now has an assured place in the USAF. Just to prove a point the ANG A-10s of the 175 TFG took part in "Gunsmoke '91" - a biennial world-wide tactical bombing and gunnery meet, sponsored by Tactical Air Command. Facing competition from an AFRes A-10 unit plus regular units equipped with the F-15E, F-16, F-111 and A-7 flown by ANG, AFRes and TAC units, 175 TFG came out on top.

RIGHT: *The Grumman F-14 Tomcat was ordered as a replacement for the F-111B, which had been cancelled in 1968. An order was placed for six prototypes (later increased to 12) and the first aircraft took to the air on 21st December 1970. The F-14 is a variable geometry air superiority fighter. It has wings which sweep from 200 to 680, enabling the aircraft to optimise its flying characteristics according to the aspect of the role being flown. Wings would be set at 200 for take off and landing as well as loitering during Combat Air Patrol (CAP), while high speed dash would be more efficient at the 680 sweep. An on-board computer can control the wing sweep to optimise it to the aircraft's speed during combat manoeuvres, although the angle can also be manually operated by the pilot.*

The F-14 Tomcat is armed with a 20mm Vulcan cannon fitted on the left side of the forward fuselage. Four AIM-54A Phoenix AAMs can be fitted in semi-recessed position under the fuselage, with another one under each wing. The Phoenix is a highly sophisticated AAM with a range in excess of 150 miles and a speed of Mach 5 plus, designed specifically for the Tomcat. A pair of Sparrow AAMs or Sidewinders can also be fitted to a pylon under each wing.

The Tomcat in the foreground is from VF-33, while another from VF-102 is being prepared for the loading of AIM-54 Phoenix and Sparrow AAMs. These two Squadrons are on board USS America and provide fighter cover for the carrier group.

LEFT: *A Tomcat of VF-33, based on USS Kennedy, flies fighter cover for a pair of EA-6 Prowlers refuelling from a KC-135 over Saudi Arabia while bound for Iraq.*

The only export order for the F-14 Tomcat was for 80 by the Shah of Iran. Following his overthrow the last aircraft, which was being used for additional trials, was retained.

The US Navy has upgraded 200 of its F-14As to the F-14B model (originally known as F-14+) by the fitting of the GE F-110 engines which give 30 per cent more power. In addition, the avionics have been upgraded and the cockpit reworked. The US Navy has also ordered 55 of the F-14D, which is further enhanced with digital systems.

ABOVE: *An F-14 Tomcat from VF-33 is launched from USS* America, *aided by a steam catapult. During the Gulf War the Tomcats flew numerous fighter cover missions for the strike aircraft flying into Iraq. Additional fighter cover was also given to her sister squadron on USS* America- *VF-102 – aircraft from which were used regularly as a photo reconnaissance platform using the Tactical Air Reconnaissance Pod System (TARPS) for battle damage assessment and the monitoring of enemy troop/equipment movements, in addition to their normal role as fighters.*

RIGHT: *This photo was taken by an F-14 Tomcat of VF-102, based on USS* America, *using TARPS. It was taken on 2nd March '91 for damage assessment of the Umm Al Aysh satellite communications site which had been the subject of an Allied attack.*

61

ABOVE: *A US Navy F-14A Tomcat based at the Pacific Missile Test Range at Point Mugu fires a Hughes AIM-54C Phoenix long range air-to-air missile.*

RIGHT: *A US Navy F-14A Tomcat from VF-1 escorts a pair of Soviet Air Force Tupolev Tu-16 "Badger F" electronic gathering aircraft. Western exercises, especially the larger ones, have tended in the past to attract the Soviet electronic monitoring and reconnaissance aircraft, thus providing tasks for the fighter aircraft. It will be interesting to see how these monitoring flights change in future years with the new era of good relations.*

RIGHT: *A Tomcat of VF-102 "Diamondbacks" climbs vertically under the power of its pair of 9,480kg Pratt & Whitney TF30-P-412A turbofans, which can develop 20,900lb with re-heat. It has a maximum speed of Mach 2.34 at altitude and a service ceiling of 56,000ft.*

LEFT: *A Grumman F-14A Tomcat of VF-102 "Diamondbacks" climbs away from USS America. Visible are the front pair of four Phoenix AAMs under the fuselage and long-range fuel tanks under the air intakes. On the bottom of each of the underwing pylons is a Sparrow AAM plus a Sidewinder on the side.*

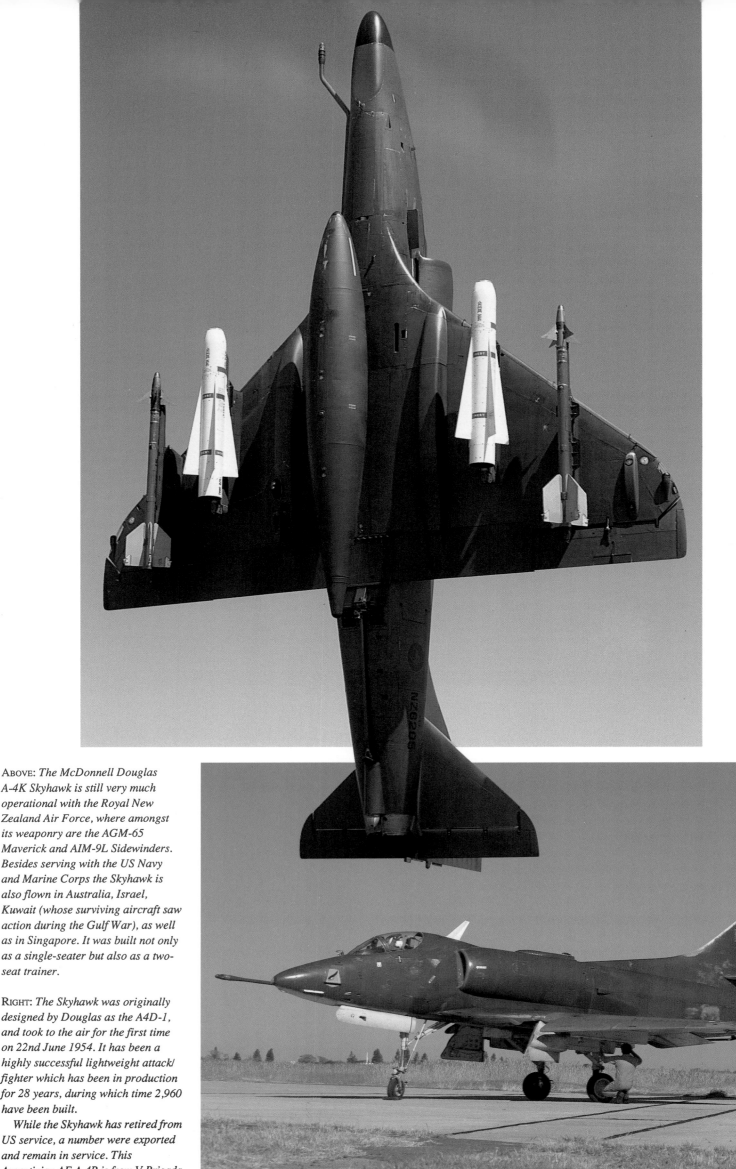

ABOVE: *The McDonnell Douglas A-4K Skyhawk is still very much operational with the Royal New Zealand Air Force, where amongst its weaponry are the AGM-65 Maverick and AIM-9L Sidewinders. Besides serving with the US Navy and Marine Corps the Skyhawk is also flown in Australia, Israel, Kuwait (whose surviving aircraft saw action during the Gulf War), as well as in Singapore. It was built not only as a single-seater but also as a two-seat trainer.*

RIGHT: *The Skyhawk was originally designed by Douglas as the A4D-1, and took to the air for the first time on 22nd June 1954. It has been a highly successful lightweight attack/ fighter which has been in production for 28 years, during which time 2,960 have been built.*

While the Skyhawk has retired from US service, a number were exported and remain in service. This Argentinian AF A-4P is from V Brigada Aerea based at Reynolds Air Base.

BELOW: *Much overseas interest was shown in the Phantom and the first order came from the British Government. This was in the form of an order for 52 F-4Ks, including four development YF-4Ks for the Royal Navy, which were known as the Phantom FG.1 in service. As part of the negotiation the RN Phantoms were fitted with the Rolls Royce Spey engines in place of the GE J79, as well as with a quantity of British built equipment and instrumentation.*

In 1978 the last RN Squadron disbanded as a result of the Government's decision to withdraw forces from east of Suez and the scrapping of the aircraft carriers. The remaining Phantom FG.1s were then transferred to the RAF to form Nos 43 and 111 Squadrons. This Phantom FG.1 of No. 111 Squadron can be seen firing its 20mm M61 Vulcan cannon contained in the SUU-23/A pod. This is a Gatling-type cannon which is capable of firing 6,000 rounds per minute.

ABOVE: *The McDonnell XF-4H-1 Phantom II made its first flight on 27 May 1958 and was destined to become a highly successful, all-round military combat aircraft. It was originally designed as a carrier-based strike/fighter for the US Navy. When production ended in March 1979 a total of 5,057 had been completed at St. Louis, with 11 sets of components and 127 licence production aircraft for Japan. A further 16, the last production batch, were for Iran, although these were not completed or delivered for political reasons. A number of world records were broken by the Phantom, including the world absolute altitude of 98,537ft (30,034m) in December 1958 and the world absolute speed of 1,606.3 mph (2,585km/h), or Mach 2.6, in December 1961. These brought the Phantom fully into the limelight.*

While deliveries of F-4As, F-4Bs and RF-4Bs were being made to the US Navy and USMC, the USAF ordered 583 F-4Cs, followed by a further order for 505 RF-4Cs. Production for the US forces progressed, with developments in engine and equipment producing a range of variants.

Besides being an impressive fighter the Phantom proved to be an effective bomber, which could carry a combination of underwing stores up to a total weight of 12,980lb (5,888kg). The events in Vietnam meant that demand for the Phantom was high, and production peaked at 72 aircraft per month in 1967. Today, the Phantom is in decline in the US forces, where it is being replaced by the F/A-18 within the US Navy and Marine Corps and the F-16 in the USAF.

ABOVE: *All Fighter Squadrons of the Royal Air Force regularly deploy for their Armament Practice Camp (APC) at RAF Akrotiri on Cyprus. Fighter pilots are required to obtain or renew their Allied Command Europe (ACE) gunnery qualification. This they must achieve by scoring a certain number of hits on a target banner towed behind a target tug. Before loading, each of the shells are painted with a coloured ink – a* different colour for each aircraft. Each aircrew is then required to fly an attack profile and fire at the target. The target tug then returns to Akrotiri and the scores are checked. Representative of the size of the vital section of an aircraft, a target banner can be seen draped over a Phantom from No. 111 Squadron. Also visible are the holes which are stained with ink to enable the instructors to credit the appropriate pilot. The RAF Phantoms are in the final process of being replaced by the Tornado F.3.

The target tug is also undergoing a replacement. For many years the facility has been operated by Canberras of 100 Sqn on detachment from RAF Wyton. These are now being replaced by the Hawk T.1.

RIGHT: *When the British Government cancelled the P.1154 in 1965 the RAF had already shown interest in the Phantom as the Hunter replacement. This resulted in a further order for 118 of the F-4M, which was designated Phantom FGR.2 and included a pair of YF-4Ms.*

In RAF service the Phantom operated in the reconnaissance role, for which it was fitted with an EMI pod under the fuselage. In the early days of the RAF Phantom it was frequently required to operate in support of the Army, carrying a variety of bombs and able to use the SUU-23/A to devastating effect. Gradually the attack role was dropped and the Phantom has been employed almost exclusively as a fighter within RAF service.

Following the Falklands War, Phantoms were deployed to RAF Stanley and then later, when it was completed, transferred to RAF Mount Pleasant. This out-of-area operation upset RAF plans as there were insufficient Victor tankers available to deploy capacity to the Falklands – besides which RAF Stanley would have been too small. A number of Hercules were hastily modified during the Falklands War and a flight of them have become a permanent feature in the Falklands.

This Phantom FGR.2 from No. 1453 Flight is equipped with a pair of Sidewinder AAMs and can be seen receiving fuel from an RAF Hercules C.1P of 1312 Flight while on CAP in the South Atlantic.

The deployment of the Phantoms to the Falklands created a further major problem for the RAF, whose fighter cover was already stretched with the slipping of the Tornado ADV programme. As a stopgap 15 ex-US Navy F-4Js were bought. These remained as standard US airframes with the J79 engines and without various modifications such as the fin-tip ESM pod. The first stopgap Phantom F4J(UK) was delivered in 1984 and the last retired in 1991.

It is intended that the Phantom will be retired from RAF service by the end of 1992, but the decision to replace 1453 Flight with the Tornado has not yet been made.

RIGHT: *Besides the US services, the RAF and the German Air Force, the Phantom has been used to equip a number of countries including Egypt, Greece (F-4E illustrated), Iran, Israel, Japan (who built them under licence), South Korea, Spain and Turkey.*

LEFT: *The Ford Aerospace/Raytheon AIM-9 Sidewinder has become one of the most prolific AAMs. It originally entered service in 1956 and relies on an infra-red signature to hit its target, much as the snake of the same name does to catch its prey.*

Over the years a number of improvements have been made to the warhead, range and sensitivity of the seeker head.

The AIM-9 shown here is also being loaded onto an RAF Phantom and is being handled by ground-crew wearing full NBC clothing.

RIGHT: *The German Air Force took an interest in the Phantom and ordered 88 of the RF-4E. These were ordered to replace the RF-104G in the reconnaissance role and the first aircraft was delivered on 19th January 1971.*

This RF-4E from AKG.51 is in the landing configuration, with the arrester hook deployed. It also has the flaps open on the flare dispenser located directly above the engine exhaust. The flares would be fired when the pilot considered he was under attack from a heat-seeking missile: the object being to use the intense heat of the flare to distract the missile.

LEFT: *A Raytheon AIM-7 Sparrow Air-to-Air Missile (AAM) ready for loading onto an RAF Phantom. The first of the Sparrow family of AAMs originally entered service with the USAF in 1958, used a beam-riding guidance system and has now been withdrawn. The Mk 2 was designed to use an active guidance but was cancelled.*

The third and current version uses a semi-active radar. Using the radar returns from the launch aircraft, the missile is able to home in on the target aircraft. Powered by a solid propellant rocket motor, the Sparrow will accelerate to its cruise speed of Mach 4 and has a maximum range of 62 miles. It is the standard weapon for all US Military Phantoms as well as for most export customers. It is also the standard weapon for the F-104S of the Italian Air Force, for the F-14, F-15, F-16 and F/A-18.

British Aerospace have developed the design as the Sky Flash, and Selenia of Italy have produced the Aspide. Further variants are used as a Surface-to-Air Missile (SAM) from ships as Sea Sparrow, and from land as Land Sparrow. The missile is due to be superseded by the Advanced Medium Range Air-to-Air Missile (AMRAAM) in the near future.

LEFT: *The German Air Force were plesed with the performance of the RF-4E Phantom which resulted in an order for 175 of the F-4F variant to replace some of the Starfighters in the strike and interceptor roles.*

RIGHT: *The LTV A-7 Corsair II was designed for the US Navy to a requirement for an aircraft which could carry double the warload of the A-4 Skyhawk for twice the distance. First flown on 27th September 1965, the A-7 entered active service when VA-147 flew into action from USS* Ranger *in the Gulf of Tonkin.*

Impressed with the potential of the A-7, the USAF ordered a quantity which were powered by the more powerful Allison TF30-P-8, which developed 15,000lb of thrust, and these were designated A-7D. This variant also incorporated a number of advanced avionics for navigation and all-weather weapon delivery. In addition a 20mm M-61 Vulcan gun was fitted in the fuselage.

The A-7 has now been withdrawn from the regular air force but still flies with the Air National Guard. This A-7D of 107 TFS is operated by the Michigan ANG.

RIGHT: *The LTV (later to become Vought) A-7 Corsair II has only seen limited operation outside US Forces. Only two countries purchased the aircraft. One was Greece, which purchased 60 A-7Hs plus 5 TA-7H two-seat trainers. The other was Portugal, which took delivery of 44 A-7Ps and 6 TA-7Cs.*

This A-7P Corsair II is from No. 302 Attack Squadron of the Portuguese Air Force based at Monte Real Air Base. While these aircraft are mainly tasked with maritime attack, the current lack of an interceptor requires the Corsair to provide fighter when necessary, in support of the Sidewinder-equipped T-38 Talon trainers. The situation is to be rectified shortly following successful negotiations to acquire a squadron of F-16s.

LEFT: *A-7Es of VA-72 from USS* John F. Kennedy *en route to Iraqi targets and armed with CBUs. The Cluster Bombs weigh 490lbs and contain 247 M-118 bomblets which are released at 500ft and will cover an area of 30,000 sq. ft. Depending on the target, a range of CBUs are available. Along with sister Squadron VA-46, the A-7s flew 722 missions and clocked over 3,000 hours during the Gulf War. Over 20 per cent of all Rockeyes CBUs dropped by the coalition forces were dropped from A-7s.*

On 23rd May 1991 the last US Navy A-7E Corsair was retired, but the aircraft may continue flying, with the possible sale of 30 aircraft to the Thai Air Force.

LEFT: *The A-7 Corsair is armed with the 20mm Vulcan gun and can also be fitted with a Sidewinder AAM on a pylon either side of the fuselage. It can carry an impressive warload totalling over 15,000lb of stores on these and the six underwing pylons. The A-7 has been involved in most recent US operations, having seen combat in Grenada, Lebanon, Libya and Panama. In January 1991 the A-7s were involved in a further major conflict when they were deployed as part of the Allied Forces in Desert Storm.*

Sidewinder AAMs are being prepared for this A-7E during Desert Storm, while bombs are already positioned by the wings ready for arming the aircraft for another mission.

ABOVE: *The US Navy A-7E has a 2,861-mile ferry range on maximum fuel, but this drops considerably during operational flying. During the Gulf War the average range was 690 nautical miles. All of these Corsair IIs from VA-72 are flying on internal fuel and are fitted with Sidewinders for self protection. Three of the aircraft are carrying four 2,000 bombs – A-7s dropped a total of 1,033 tons of iron bombs on Iraqi targets. The fourth is loaded with four of the AGM-88 HARM anti-radar missiles. These would be to provide protection from SAM sites. A-7s fired 152 HARMs against SAM and radar-controlled gun positions.*

As with most of the missions in the Gulf War, the A-7s are being topped up with fuel by a USAF KC-135. In addition a KA-6D tanker is receiving fuel. This mission must be close to the maximum range for the A-7s and it has been considered that additional fuel may be required before the A-7s are able to return to the KC-135. The KA-6D is, therefore, required to join the Corsairs.

Above: *The F-22 is the Lockheed/ Boeing/General Dynamics joint successful proposal for the Advanced Tactical Fighter requirement for the USAFs next generation of fighter to replace the F-15. In competition with the McDonnell Douglas/Northrop YF-23A, it has been designed with* *stealth technology and the ability to "super cruise" (fly supersonically without afterburner). It also has operating costs in mind, and thus offers high reliability and low maintenance. Using experience from the F-117 project, composites including thermo-plastic and thermo-* *setting graphite epoxy will probably make up 30 per cent of the airframe. The F-22 will be armed with the AMRAAM and latest Sidewinders in multiple internal weapon bays. Pylons will provide further external capacity. The USAF has a planned requirement for 750 F-22s.* *The Lockheed YF-22 made its first flight on 27th August 1990 and can be seen here flying over the Mojave Desert. Forward thinking at the design stage has included potential for the F-22 to fulfil a ground attack fighter role should this be required at a later date.*

The USAF requirement for a lightweight fighter in the 1970s generated five submissions from various manufacturers. Two designs were selected, for which orders were given to construct two prototypes of each. The aircraft were the General Dynamics YF-16 and the Northrop YF-17. Following a total of some 600 hours of flight testing between them the YF-16 was selected.

The Northrop YF-17 design was evolved from the P-530 Cobra project, and the company had spent a considerable amount of time developing these two projects without success. Meanwhile, the US Navy was studying the requirement for a low cost, lightweight multi-mission fighter. To save further large expenditure Congress directed the Navy to consider the capable YF-16 and YF-17 which already existed. McDonnell Douglas had also been working on the requirement and considered that the YF-17 was close to the Navy's needs. What was required was a substantial increase in fuel capacity to meet the range requirement plus an overall strengthening to meet the higher gross weight and the rigours of carrier operations. As a result the two manufacturers teamed together.

The US Navy became very interested in the project, and after a little further modification an order was given for 11 prototypes, which were given the designation F-18 Hornet. The aircraft made its maiden flight on 18th November 1978.

The F/A-18 Hornets were heavily involved in Desert Storm. This particular US Marine Corps Hornet from the VMFA(AW)-451 is armed with a pair of Sidewinder AAMs on the wingtips plus a pair of Sparrow AAMs. In addition this aircraft is armed with a 20mm M-61 gun in the nose. A further four pylons are available for additional weapons or, as in this case, drop tanks. Painted under the fuselage is a dummy cockpit to confuse the enemy.

BELOW: *The F/A-18 has seen reasonable success in the export field, with the Australians purchasing 57 A/F-18As and 18 A/F-18B two-seat trainers. An order from South Korea for 12 aircraft plus 36 kits precede licence production by Samsung of 72 aircraft, which could increase if a total requirement for 300 aircraft materialises. Spain is also a major user of the Hornet, having ordered 60 EF-18As and 12 EF-18Bs.*

The Canadian Armed Forces (CAF) operate four squadrons of CF-18s in the air defence role plus another for training, with 86 CF-18As and 39 CF-18Bs. Two of the fighter squadrons regularly exercise deployment to Lahr in Germany for the rapid reinforcement of NATO.

This CF-18A is seen pulling high "G" and creating the characteristic condensation formed over the large wing root extensions. It also displays the shadow cockpit painted on the underside of the fuselage to confuse the enemy.

No. 409 Squadron was deployed from Germany to the Gulf as part of the Allied Forces.

ABOVE: *The Kuwait Air Force selected the F/A-18 Hornet in 1988 and placed an order for 40 aircraft. Following the invasion of Kuwait by Iraq, the US Navy directed McDonnell Douglas to continue with the order and the programme has remained on schedule. In January '91 the first three Hornets arrived in Kuwait, and they will be used to restore the country's full air defence capability as well as replacing the A-4KU Skyhawk and Mirage F.1.*

ABOVE: *A trolley containing four Sidewinder AAMs is positioned on the flight deck of USS* America *for the awaiting F/A-18 Hornets of VFA-82 and VFA-86. During Desert Storm the Navy and Marine Hornets flew over 10,000 sorties and clocked up in excess of 25,000 hours, with only a single aircraft lost in combat. Over 18 million pounds of ordnance were delivered, which included HARM, Iron bombs, Walleye (TV guided) bombs, Laser guided bombs, Maverick (TV guided missiles) and rockets, as well as the Stand off Land Attack Missile (SLAM). In addition, for protection the Hornets carried the Sidewinder and Sparrow AAMs.*

Desert Storm got off to a good start for VF-81. Flying as part of a flight of four aircraft from USS

Saratoga and tasked to attack H-3 – an airfield inside Iraq – the aircraft were each armed with a pair of AIM-9M Sidewinders and AIM-7M Sparrows as well as their M61 gun. In addition, three of the aircraft carried 3 Mk.84 2,000lb General Purpose (GP) bombs and an ALQ-167 pod to counter the SA-6 SAM threat. The fourth aircraft was launched as a spare and was loaded with four of the 2,000lb bombs.

The four Hornets were well into the mission, only 35 miles from the target, and were selecting the air-to-ground master mode ready for the final attack, when a message from an AEW E-2 Hawkeye monitoring the mission called "Bandits on your nose, 15". Flying as two pairs, both wingmen reset their master mode to

air-to-air and the first missile was fired as soon as the target was acquired. Lt Cdr Mark "MRT" Fox watched the MiG-21 closely and thought that his Sidewinder had failed to track the target so reselected for Sparrow and fired again. Therefore the Sidewinder impacted, setting fire to the Iraqi fighter, briefly followed by the Sparrow. Meanwhile, the other Hornet piloted by Lt Nick "Mongo" Mongillo had successfully tracked and hit the other incoming MiG-21 with a Sparrow. With the Bogeys downed, all four aircraft reverted to the air-to-ground master mode and successfully completed the attack on the airfield, returning to the USS Saratoga undamaged and without further incident.

BELOW LEFT: *An F/A-18C Hornet on full afterburner is about to be catapulted down the deck of USS* America. *In recent years all the aircraft markings have been toned down to what is known as shadow markings, where everything is reduced to two tones of grey. This is in stark contrast to the '60s and '70s, when all US Navy aircraft sported highly colourful squadron markings.*

Colour has, however, achieved a toe in the door once more, with each squadron permitted to paint one aircrafts markings in colour as a flagship. Perhaps now that tension from the East/West Cold War is receeding, some of the old traditions can return.

This particular F/A-18C Hornet about to launch is the personal aircraft of Commander of Air Group (CAG) CVW-1 aboard USS America: *Captain Paul Cash.*

LEFT: *The same F/A-18C Hornet returns for the arrester landing. The aircraft is initially guided in by air traffic control until the ship is well within visual distance. From then on the pilot must judge his approach, which will be at an angle to the moving ship. There will also be turbulence at its stern – just at the most critical point of the landing. To help the pilot a system of lights indicates the correct angle of approach as well as track. Although the hook is deployed and there are a number of cables on the deck, there is no firm guarantee that the aircraft will connect. This means that each touchdown must be assumed to be a roller landing, with throttle opened ready for immediate take-off. Only when the pilot feels the aircraft being pulled out from under him does he know that he has fully landed.*

Once landed, the emphasis changes into an organised panic to clear the aircraft away from the landing area and enable the next aircraft to land. To reduce the space required, the Hornet has wings that can be folded along a point outboard of the pylons. Even so, the deck becomes extremely crowded and it requires a great deal of planning, communication and accurate marshalling to ensure that launches and landings progress smoothly.

The F/A-18 Hornet is operated from 12 aircraft carriers and 15 Navy and Marine Corps air stations. The night attack variants – F/A-18C single-seat and F/A-18D two-seat – commenced delivery in October 1989. They are equipped with thermal imaging navigation and night vision systems which give the same capability at night that current aircraft have by day. Further development is planned for the F/A-18E and F upgrades.

RIGHT: *Lt Eric "Hitch" Rasmussen of VFA-86 relaxes ready for take off from USS* America. *The markings below the cockpit indicate that he has fourteen Desert Storm attack plus two anti radar missions to his credit.*

During the catapult launch of the A/F-18 Hornet, the pilot will hold the pair of handles located above the rear view mirrors. The reason for this is that it is considered safer than accepting accidental incorrect control inputs induced during the high acceleration of the launch sequence on the pilot. The Hornet has been designed to fly for the first few seconds hands off.

ABOVE: *The McDonnell Douglas AV-8B Harrier II is a development of the British Aerospace Harrier GR.3, which is operated by the RAF, and the AV-8A Harrier of the USMC. With 102 AV-8A/TAV-8As in service, the USMC found this V/STOL aircraft to be very capable operationally, although it was limited in carrying capacity. Initially the British Government agreed to a joint study to decide on a replacement, but it was decided that the RAF requirement was not compatible and resulted in the British withdrawal. McDonnell Douglas continued with the programme and two AV-8As were converted to become the TAV-8B prototypes. The first took to the air on 9th November 1978.*

The first AV-8B proper flew on the 5th November 1981 and is a substantial improvement on its predecessor. It has a larger supercritical wing with extra fuel capacity, which is largely constructed from graphite epoxy, with enlarged trailing edge flaps and drooped ailerons. The 21,500lb Rolls Royce Pegasus Mk.803 was replaced by the Pegasus F403, which develops 23,800lbs. Lift improvement was further improved by containing the exhaust gases as they rebound from the ground. It is also fitted with advanced avionics systems to aid the pilot, including an Angle Rate Bombing System (ARBS). The pilot

locks this onto the target and the computer calculates and displays the weapon delivery data for the pilot on the Head Up Display (HUD).

This AV-8B Harrier II is from VMA-231 based at Cherry Point and is equipped with a pair of Sidewinder AAMs plus a Mk.82 Snakeye bomb on each of the other four pylons. VMA-231 is one of eight USMC attack squadrons which are equipped with the AV-8B. A further training squadron exists with a number of TA-V8Bs and AV-8Bs.

RIGHT: *The Spanish Navy initially ordered six AV-8As and two TAV-8As followed an additional five AV-8As. With the development of the AV-8B for the USMC, Spain became a logical potential customer for the new variant. In 1978 the Spanish Government ordered a further five Harriers, or Matadors as they were known locally, for their Navy.*

In 1983 the Spanish Navy ordered 12 AV-8Bs initially to operated alongside the EAV-8As, but eventually replace them. They were delivered during 1987-8 and are operated by 9 Squadron as illustrated here.

An additional order was placed on behalf of the Italian Navy for 12 aircraft, to which a further 10 was later.

ABOVE: *Whilst the AV-8B Harrier II was equipped with an extremely accurate ABRS, it was limited to daylight operations. The introduction of the Night Attack Harrier resolved this and it now has a full 24-hour capability.*

This is the prototype of the Night Attack Harrier and is armed with a pair of the laser-guided Maverick AGMs.

The Super Etendard suddenly became the centre of attention when, on 4th May 1982, a pair of the aircraft from 2nd Escuadrilla – the Argentinian Naval Attack Squadron operating out of Rio Grande – each launched their single Exocet missiles at the British Task Force. While one of the missiles fell harmlessly into the sea at the end of its flight, the other struck HMS Sheffield *at an angle amidships and continued to the stern. Fortunately the missile did not explode, but the effect of the mass of the 1,455lb missile hitting the ship at nearly 700mph, together with burning fuel and explosive caused extensive damage, casualties and eventual loss of the ship. This mission was repeated on the 25th May, causing the loss of the* Atlantic Conveyor *and virtually all of her contents. Again, the second missile was to fall harmlessly.*

This was at a time when the Argentinian Navy was equipped with only five of the 14 Super Etendards ordered as well as only five Exocet missiles. The aircraft were so new to the Argentinians that pilots had flown little over the 45 hours of basic training undertaken in France, no tactical training missions had been flown and the attack and radar computer software had not been upgraded to integrate the Exocet. One of the Super Etendards had to be cannibalised to keep the others flying. With the limited resources available, the aircraft and their crews wreaked major damage on the British Task Force.

All 14 of the Super Etendards have now been delivered to Argentina and they are back at their normal base at Comandante Espora. They can be fitted with the Matra Magic II for self-defence.

LEFT: *The Dassault Super Etendard was designed to replace the Etendard IVM of the French Navy following the cancellation of the Jaguar M. The Super Etendard was developed directly from the IVM, two of the prototypes being converted from existing airframes, the first of which made its maiden flight on 28th October 1974.*

The Super Etendard is powered by the Atar 8K-50, which produces over 10 per cent more thrust than that of the IVM while burning less fuel. It is equipped with the Agave multi-role radar, which provides data for the air-to-air and air-to-ground/sea role as well as having a very accurate navigation and attack system. The Super Etendard is also fitted with a modified wing which provides a better lift factor.

A total of 71 Super Etendards have been delivered to the French Navy to operate from the carriers Foch and Clemenceau. They are fitted with a pair of 30mm cannon internally and can carry a pair of Matra 550 Magic AAMs for self defence. They can also carry up to 3,500lb of bombs for ground targets, or the Exocet missile for the anti-ship role.

RIGHT: *The Mirage III has served with the French and numerous other Air Forces around the world in considerable numbers. The aircraft was designed to meet a requirement for a small supersonic interceptor. It first flew on 25th June 1955, the French Air Force rapidly became interested and ordered 10 pre-production aircraft. Shortly after the first pre-production fighter flew the aircraft was ordered into production as the Mirage IIIC. A two-seat trainer variant, designated the Mirage IIIB, was also ordered. This was later followed by the IIIE fighter bomber and the IIIR reconnaissance variants, as well as a further trainer in the form of the IIID.*

A number of sub-variants were also constructed for export production in France as well as licence manufacture in Australia and Switzerland. Israel ordered and paid for a simplified variant which became the Mirage 5, but due to political decisions these were not delivered. As a result Israel built her own Mirage III known as the Dagger, and their interpretation of the Mirage 5 became the Kfir.

The Argentinian Air Force took delivery of two new IIIDAs and 17 IIIEAs, and added 19 surplus IIICJs and IIIBJs from Israel and 10 5Ps from Peru. Israel also supplies a number of the single- and two-seat IAI Daggers.

Now looking its age, this Argentinian Mirage IIICJ is from Escuadron 55 and is based at El Plumerillo Air Base.

RIGHT: *This Mirage IIIRDP from No. 5 Squadron of the Pakistani Air Force is based at Rafiqui and is the reconnaissance variant of the Mirage III family. The Mirage IIIR can be fitted with five OMERA Type 31 cameras or the SAT Cyclope infrared package. This particular example of the export variant can be seen fitted with the Sidewinder AAM.*

ABOVE: *The Mirage 50 is a further development of the Mirage 5, incorporating features from the Mirage F.1, 2000 and 4000. In addition to improvements in the avionics and radar, the Mirage 50 is fitted with the Atar 9K-50 from the Mirage F.1, which gives it a 20 per cent increase in thrust over the Mirage III. It is also fitted with canards which improve the handling characteristics.*

This Mirage 50CU "Pantera" is one of 14 single-seat and two training two-seaters operated by the Chilean Air Force.

BELOW: *The Dassault Mirage 5 is a simplified version of the Mirage III. It uses the same basic airframe but the electronics have been reduced to those specifically required for the attack role. Additional fuel has been fitted as well as under-wing stores pylons.*

This Mirage 5PA of the Pakistani Air Force is one of 58 purchased along with two 5DPD trainers. Dassault saw reasonable success with exports of the Mirage 5, with additional sales made to Belgium, Columbia, Egypt, Gabon, Libya, Peru and Zaire, as well as to the French Air Force.

LEFT: *Dassault designed the original Mirage back in the early '50s and it has remained the family name, although the design has changed radically over the years.*

The Mirage F.1 was designed as the replacement for the Mirage III and 5 series of aircraft. This was a private venture which first flew on 23rd December 1966, and although it crashed a few months later it showed sufficient potential for a further three prototypes to be ordered by the French Government.

Deliveries of the Mirage F.1 swept wing interceptor commenced on 14th March 1973 as the F.1C, with the F.1B being the two-seat trainer. A total of 186 were built.

The French Air Force Mirage F.1CR from ER1/33, photographed in the Gulf, is armed with a pair of the Matra R.530 Magic AAMs and the Ramora jammer pod for self defence, together with a pair of bombs under each wing. Operating in the reconnaissance role, the Mirage F.1CRs provided a useful function for Allied Forces by mapping the Iraqi forward positions using their SLAR pods.

The Mirage is in formation with a Jaguar from EC2/11, also fitted with the Ramora jammer pod and with four 1000lb bombs. Both aircraft types comprised part of the Allied Forces taking part in Desert Storm, or l' operation Daguet, as it was known by the French.

RIGHT: *This French Air Force Mirage F.1C from EC1/12 has been painted in yellow and black stripes for the annual Tiger Meet. Although France is not part of NATO her armed forces join in a number of exercises and functions as a guest.*

BELOW: *A Royal Jordanian Air Force Mirage F.1CJ of No. 25 Squadron is marshalled out for a training exercise.*

In addition to the F.1CJs the RJAF took delivery of 17 of the F.1EJ for the attack role plus two F.1BJs for training. Jordan has now ordered 12 Mirage 2000CJM interceptors, and on delivery will transfer the F.1CJs to the attack role.

LEFT: *A Fuerza Aerea Ecuatoriana (Ecuador Air Force) Mirage F.1JA formates with a SEPECAT Jaguar and IAI Kfir C2. The Mirages, of which 16 F.1JA and 2 F.1JE were delivered, are used in the interceptor role. The two-seaters are for training, although they retain the capabilities of the fighter and could be used in that role if required. The 10 Jaguar ES are for the strike role, as are the similar number of Kfir C2s. The four Jaguars lost in accidents over the years are to replaced by three refurbished ex-RAF Jaguar GR.1s. A pair of Jaguar EB and a Kfir TC2 are used for training.*

Futher exports of the Mirage F.1 have been made to Greece (40), Iraq (113), Kuwait (33), Libya (38), Morocco (50), South Africa (48) and Spain (73).

LEFT: *The Mirage 2000 is the current generation of the Mirage family and represents a significant increase in performance over previous models. It took to the air for the first time on 19th March 1978 and takes full advantage of the experience built up with the earlier types. It has fly-by-wire controls and extensive use is made of composite materials. It has an advanced navigation and weapon system and is fitted with a long-range radar. Its powerful Snecma M53 turbofan engines give it a Mach 2.2+ performance. It can carry a wide range of air-to-air or air-to-ground weaponry in addition to having a pair of 30mm guns mounted internally. An order for 127 was placed by the French Air Force to replace the IIIE.*

Export deliveries of the Mirage 2000 have been made to a number of countries including Abu Dhabi, Egypt, Greece, India, Jordan and Peru.

The formation of the Indian Air Force Mirage 2000H comprises of aircraft from Nos 1 and 7 Squadrons.

BELOW: *This Mirage 2000B is the trainer variant of the 2000 family which has been designed to incorporate all the roles of the single seater. It is shown here being demonstrated at Farnborough, equipped with the R550 Magic AAM to emphasise its ability to operate in either role without need for conversion.*

RIGHT: *The Mirage 2000C-RDI is the latest variant in the air defence range of the 2000 family. It is fitted with two 30mm DEFA cannon, one of which is visible just below the air intake, plus a pair of Matra Super 530D AAMs and a further pair of Matra 550 Magic AAMs. This Mirage 2000-RDI is from EC2/5, based at Orange, and was one of the French Air Force aircraft which formed part of the Allied Force during Desert Storm.*

BELOW: *The French Air Force issued a requirement for a new generation of heavy fighter. Dassault proceeded with the project, known as the Avion de Combat Futur (ACF). In 1975 this was cancelled some six months before it was due to fly. The French Government had decided to follow the current trend and revert back to the lighter fighter.*

Having proceeded so far with the ACF project Dassault, with the support of the French aircraft industry, decided to re-assess the project. Using experience gained with the ACF, they designed and built the Mirage 4000. This first flew on the 9th March 1979. This 20 tonne aircraft has been designed for the interception and low-level strike roles.

Looking like a very much scaled up Mirage 2000, the 4000 is potentially a very powerful aircraft. In the 20 tonne class, it can be seen fitted with six Matra 550 Magic AAMs. Whilst this is a potent aircraft it is yet to receive an order.

ABOVE: *The Vought Crusader first flew on 25th March 1955 and served with the US Navy initially as a supersonic fighter. They were later issued to the Marines and have flown in a number of roles. The Crusader has now been withdrawn from service in the USA.*

The Crusader was only exported to two countries. The Philippines bought 25 ex-USN F-8Hs plus a further 10 for spares. They were withdrawn in 1988 due to a combination of economics and serviceability.

The only other foreign recipient of the Crusader was the French Navy, which purchased 42 F-8E(FN)s. The first French Crusader took to the air on 11th April 1964 and was used to equip two squadrons.

The Crusader features a wing that pivots 7° to increase the angle of attack to maintain the pilot's vision during low speed flight. In addition to this the French Crusaders were fitted with extra lift enhancers to enable them to operate successfully from the smaller French carriers – the Clemenceau and the Foch. They can be armed with a pair of Matra Magic or Sidewinder AAMs on a rail either side of the fuselage. In addition the F-8 is fitted with four 20mm Colt-Browning cannon in the nose.

The last remaining F-8E(FN) unit is 12 Flotille and it is planned to commence re-equipping with the Rafale M in 1998.

RIGHT: *The Dassault-Breguet/ Dornier Alpha Jet is an international collaboration project for an advanced trainer for the French and German Air Forces. The project also incorporated the Germans' additional requirement for a battlefield reconnaissance and light strike aircraft. This has resulted in two variants which retain much in common.*

The French variant was the first to fly, on the 26th October 1973. As a strike/support aircraft the Alpha Jet can carry a range of weapons on its four pylons. It is shown here equipped with the Aerospatiale Exocet anti-shipping missile and a pair of inert Matra Magic AAMs.

In service with the French Air Force, it has replaced the T-33s and Mystere IVs and is in the process of taking over from the last of the Fouga Magisters. The Germans have used it to replace the T-33 and G-91.

In addition to the French Air Force, which has 176, and the German, with 175, the Alpha Jet is operated by Belgium (33), Cameroun (6), Egypt (45), Ivory Coast (6), Morocco (23+), Nigeria (24), Qatar (6) and Togo (5)

RIGHT: *The Dassault Rafale has been designed as the replacement for the various intercept and ground-attack aircraft currently flown by the French Air Force and Navy. Four development aircraft have been ordered by the French Government as a follow on from the Rafale A Technology Demonstrator, which took to the air for the first time on 4th July 1986.*

Three variants of the basic Rafale airframe are planned. The C (illustrated) is to be the interceptor to replace the Mirage F.1 and 2000, with the B as the two-seat trainer. The M is the Navy version to replace the F-8FN Crusader. Each will retain a common engine (2 x SNECMA M-88), weapon delivery and navigation system, and will carry the MICA and APACHE missiles. The Rafale is planned to enter service in 1997.

This prototype Rafale C is fitted with a pair of Matra R.550 Magic AAMs.

ABOVE: *The Mitsubishi F-1 is based on the T-2 supersonic trainer. It was built for the Japanese Air Self-Defence Force (JASDF) as a close support fighter. The prototype F-1 was converted from a production T-2 and was first flown on 3rd June 1975. The prototype retained the rear cockpit of the T-2 and was fitted with the fire control and extra test equipment.*

The production Mitsubishi F.1 basically retains the design of the T-2, although the F-1 was fitted with more appropriate electronics plus a 20mm JM.61 cannon. In addition, four hard points had been built into the wing which are capable of carrying up to 12 500lb bombs. The F-1 can carry the Sidewinder for the fighter role or a variety of other weapons depending on the mission requirements. Over 70 F-1s have been delivered to the JASDF.

RIGHT: *It is planned that the JASDF Mitsubishi F-1 will be replaced in the late '90s by the Mitsubishi SX-3. This is based on the General Dynamics F-16 and it is thought that the requirement for the SX-3, which is also intended to replace the Phantom, may increase from 130 to approach 200.*

ABOVE: *The IAI Kfir came into being as a result of the French Government refusing to supply the 50 Mirage 5Js for which the Israelis had already paid. This was as a result of the 1967 Six-Day War. Israel built several interim types based on the Mirage III and these were powered by either the J79 or Atar.*

Looking similar to the Mirage 5, the Kfir emerged from the veil of secrecy in April 1975. It is a combination of the basic airframe with a US J79 engine and Israeli avionics. The shorter and fatter dimensions of the J79 are reflected in the shape of the Kfir fuselage, and the adoption of this engine has improved fuel consumption. In July 1976 the existence of the Kfir C2 was revealed. The canards fitted to the air intakes mark an obvious external modification for recognition purposes.

RIGHT: *The Colombian Air Force is another recipient of the Kfir and took delivery of 10 C2s fighters and two TC2 trainers during 1989. Operated by Escuadron de Combate No. 213, the similarities can be seen in this formation with the Mirage 5COD, to which canards have been added.*

The refurbished ex-Israeli AF C2s were subsequently modified up to C7 standard.

LEFT: *In 1984, an agreement was reached between the US Navy and IAI for the loan of 12 Kfir C1s for aggressor training, with payment restricted to maintenance. The Kfirs were delivered to VF-43 at Oceana NAS and designated F-21A.*

Shortly after these F-21As were delivered a second order was placed for 13 additional aircraft, this time for the USMC. All of the USMC F-21s were operated by VMFT-401, of which one is illustrated touching down and releasing its brake' chute. These aircraft were used as a stopgap while the current types were awaited. USN F-21As have now been replaced by F-5Es and the USMC by the F-16N. The F-21As have been returned to IAI, where they have been put into storage while another customer is awaited.

BELOW: *The Kfir has been offered for export to a number of countries. Although the aircraft is of Israeli construction, US approval has to be obtained before an order is accepted because of the US engines. There have been occasions when this has caused a problem.*

The Government of Ecuador purchased 14 Kfir C2/TC2s (illustrated) to equip their Air Force. These are flown by No. 2113 Squadron primarily in the strike role. The Taiwanese Air Force has ordered 34 single- and six two-seat Kfir C7s.

LEFT: *Sweden retains her neutral standing within Europe, and has gone as far as is economically possible to keep her armed forces independent from either the East or West. The Swedish Air Force has been able to rely on SAAB to produce some impressive fighters.*

The SAAB Draken was designed in the early '50s and first took to the air on 25th October 1955. Designed to carry four Sidewinder AAMs, a total of 90 J-35As were built for the Swedish Air Force. With improvements in avionics and engines the J-35B, J-35D and J-35F variants evolved, as well as production of the SK-35 trainer and S-35E reconnaissance versions. Over the years nearly 550 Drakens have been supplied for the Swedish Air Force.

The J-35F was the most numerous variant and entered service in the mid-1960s. Well over 200 were delivered, but these are now being withdrawn and replaced by the J-37 Viggen, although one Wing still remains. Recently, 64 F-35Fs have been upgraded to J-35Js, and these are expected to remain operational until the mid-1990s, when the JAS-39 Gripen enters service.

Over the years the J-35F Draken has carried a number of different missiles in addition to its pair of 30mm Aden cannon. Originally they were equipped with a pair of Hughes AIM-4D and AIM-26A Falcons, which were built under licence and designated Rb28 and Rb27 respectively. These have given way to the Sidewinder AAM.

RIGHT: *Like Sweden, Austria is a neutral country, but she does not have the resources or the indigenous aircraft industry to build her own aircraft. It is, therefore, not surprising that she has turned to Sweden for a number of her requirements.*

In 1986 the first of 24 J-35OEs were delivered to provide Austria's front line fighter force, but with armament limited to one 30mm Aden cannon. These were to replace the SAAB 105OE, which have been released for the training role, although they still get tasked with patrol duties. At the time the Draken was acquired it was felt that as a neutral country, only a token fighter force would be required. As a result of the troubles in Yugoslavia, which have resulted in a number of incursions, the Austrian Government has decided to purchase a quantity of air-to-air missiles.

Yet another neutral country to operate the Draken was Finland, which took delivery of a number of

variants as well as kits for local assembly. Currently about 40 Drakens remain operational. Although not neutral, Denmark took initial delivery of 20 of the A.35XD Draken in 1970, plus 11 of the Sk.35XD trainers and 20 of the S.35XD reconnaissance variants.

RIGHT: *The SAAB Viggen is a powerful illustration of the Swedish resolve to remain a neutral country. It was on the 8th February 1967 when the first of seven prototype Viggens thundered down the runway for the first time. Initial deliveries were of the AJ-37 strike variant, which replaced the Lansen in that role, although it was assigned fighter duties as a secondary role. Deliveries began in 1978 of the first of 149 JA-37 fighter variants of the Viggen to the Swedish Air Force. It is optimised for the interceptor role, being fitted with the more powerful Volvo Flygmotor RM8B turbofan as well as with a highly sophisticated set of pilot aids. The JA-37 is armed with a powerful 30mm Oerlikon KCA cannon as well as the Skyflash (Rb71) and Sidewinder (Rb24) AAMs.*

As part of the Swedish defence planning the Viggens have been designed to be able to take off and land in short distances. In time of tension this would allow the aircraft to be deployed on numerous off-airfield sites and to use roads as runways.

Additional variants are the SH-37 and SF-37 maritime and overland reconnaissance, and the SK-37 two-seat trainer.

RIGHT: *The SAAB-Scania JAS.39 Gripen is the latest design to emerge from the Swedish company. As with the Viggen, the Gripen has been designed as a multi-role aircraft to replace the Draken and Viggen from the mid-1990s. A total of 140 have been ordered for the Swedish Air Force and this quantity will include 15 two-seat trainers.*

The prototype first flew on 14th September 1988 and is shown fitted with a pair of Sidewinder (Rb24) AAMs. As with the Viggen, the Gripen is designed to operate from 800m airstrips such as roads. The turnaround maintenance has been designed to be simple, capable of being easily handled by conscripts.

ABOVE: *A unique formation of types designed and built by the Soviet manufacturer Mikoyan-Gurevich and operated by the Indian Air Force. In the foreground is a MiG-21M from No. 101 Squadron led by a MiG-23MF from No. 224 Squadron. This in turn is led by a MiG-29 from No. 223 Squadron and a MiG-27M from No. 9 Squadron, and the whole echelon is led by a MiG-25 from No. 102 Squadron.*

RIGHT: *This MiG-21 was operated by the Afghanistan Air Force and during the '80s flew alongside the Soviet Air Force units then based in that country. With the withdrawal of the Soviets, who had been supporting the increasingly unpopular Communist Government, the Afghanistan AF suffered a drop in morale. This resulted in a number of desertions, as with the pilot of this MiG-21, who defected to Pakistan on 29th October 1989.*

LEFT: *The Mikoyan-Gurevich MiG-21 evolved during the mid-1950s from lessons learned during the Korean War. A requirement for a fast, basic airframe with minimal equipment and only the minimum weaponry was considered desirable. Several variations were test flown, with the E-5 flying in 1955, leading up to the E-6. From this was developed the E-66, but it lacked power. A few were accepted by the Soviet Air Force under the designation MiG-21 for trials. The arrival of increased power in the MiG-21F gave the aircraft an acceptable performance and production commenced, with deliveries being made to the Warsaw Pact countries, as well as exports to Finland and India and licence production in China. The fighter variant was code named "Fishbed" by NATO, while the two-seat trainer was known as "Mongol".*

This MiG-21PF in Soviet Air Force markings is a limited all-weather variant which was fitted with a radar in the nose cone. It was normally fitted with one pod-mounted twin barrel 23mm gun plus up to four K-13 AAMs. These missiles were code named "Atoll" and were similar to the early American AIM-9B Sidewinder.

RIGHT: *The MiG-21M is a development of the FL model. It has a redesigned, deeper dorsal fairing which contains fuel. It also has additional pylons for weapons or stores, including fuel tanks. The ability to carry extra weapons give the MiG-21M an attack capability in addition to its original fighter role.*

These Indian Air Force Mig-21Ms of 101 Squadron are also painted in various exotic colour schemes.

RIGHT: *The Indian Air Force is one of a number of countries outside the Warsaw Pact to operate the MiG-21. A number of the various MiG-21 variants operated by the Indian Air Force were supplied direct from the Soviet Union, but a production line was established by Hindustan Aeronautics and several hundred have been built locally.*

The Indian Air Force operates its own MiG-21s in a variety of exotic colour schemes which are for identification purposes in air combat training. These MiG-21FLs are from 8 Squadron.

ABOVE: *The MiG-21 has proved to be the Soviets' most successful aircraft in terms of quantities built, with examples having been used by at least 38 countries including all members of the Warsaw Pact. In addition it has been operated by a large number of countries around the world and further production has been undertaken in China and India.*

The Czechoslovak Air Force has been a major operator of the MiG-21 "Fishbed" and has even had its own production line. Until recently nearly 300 examples have operated in the interceptor role but many are now in the process of being retired.

RIGHT: *The MiG-21bis has become the standard export variant of the family. The examples illustrated here are from 4 Squadron of the Indian Air Force and are also painted in the highly colourful identification markings.*

ABOVE: *The prototype MiG-23 was first displayed at the 1967 Aviation Day flypast at Domodedovo, and entered service with the Soviet Air Force in the early '70s. The MiG-23 is a variable geometry, multi-role aircraft with a number of sub-variants for specific missions.*

This is a Polish Air Force MiG-23MF interceptor of the 28th Fighter Aviation Regiment on a deployment exercise, during which they were operating from roads.

LEFT: *The MiG-23 has a somewhat complex undercarriage system, giving it a rough terrain landing capability.*

RIGHT: *The MiG-23 is supplied to most of the Warsaw Pact countries as well as to a number of those outside it. With the break up of the Soviet Union it is possible that operators of the eastern or western aircraft will be less clearly defined. However, in the meantime most of the Eastern European countries are trying to stabilise themselves and are unlikely to be making any major changes for a few years to come.*

This MiG-23MF, with the NATO code name of "Flogger-B", is operated by the Hungarian Air Force and can be seen landing with its wings swept forward.

ABOVE: *The Mig-23 has been exported to a number of countries outside the old Warsaw Pact, including Cuba, Ethiopia and Syria.*

The Indian Air Force operates a number of MiG-23BN "Flogger-Hs" primarily in the attack role. These MiG-23s of 10 Squadron can be seen fitted with U-16 rocket pods.

RIGHT: *The Czechoslovak Air Force operates MiG-23ML "Flogger-Gs" in the fighter role. While the majority of their air defences consist of Mig-21s, the MiG-23s and a limited number MiG-29s provide an improved capability. This variant has been lightened for the fighter role.*

LEFT: *The MiG-25, or "Foxbat" as it known by NATO, was first announced to the West in 1965, when the Soviets claimed a world air speed record of 1,441.5mph over a 1,000km closed circuit. The aircraft was then designated E-266 and had been fitted with a 2,000kg payload for the flight. Over the next few years a string of records was achieved, including an absolute height of 118,898ft.*

The MiG-25 was designed as a high performance fighter capable of intercepting the Lockheed A-11 and SR-71A. Due to concerns about the problem of heat on the aircraft structure, and the uncertainty of using titanium, construction was based primarily on welded steel. Approximately 80 per cent of the airframe weight is steel. It is estimated that some 13,000ft of seam welds and 1.4 million spot welds are incorporated in each MiG-25. The prototype Ye-155R first flew on 6th March 1964 and eventually entered service with the Soviet Air Force in 1972 as the MiG-25P "Foxbat A". Although a pre-production model had been seen at Tushino in 1967, the first good look the West had was when the Soviet Pilot Lt Victor Belenko defected to Japan.

This MiG-25 "Foxbat" of the Soviet Air Force is from 931 Regiment and is based at Welzow, near the German/Polish border.

BELOW: *The Indian Air Force operates a few MiG-25U "Foxbat-C" trainers.*

The MiG-25U has a redesigned nose containing a separate cockpit, but it is not fitted with radar or reconnaissance sensors.

ABOVE: *The Mig-25 has only been exported to a few countries and then only in limited quantities. It is thought that production was cut back when the emphasis changed from high level intercepts to low level. Those supplied include Algeria, Bulgaria, Libya, India, Iraq and Syria.*

This MiG-25R "Foxbat-B" is flown by 102 Sqn of the Indian Air Force and is the reconnaissance variant, which can be fitted with various reconnaissance modules including five cameras, or Side Look Airborne Radar (SLAR).

RIGHT: *The MiG-27M "Flogger-J" is a further variant of the MiG-23 and has a primary role of ground attack. It has a laser rangefinder in the nose replacing the radar, additional armour around the cockpit, and is fitted with more under-wing and fuselage hard points for the carrying of various weapons and stores. It is also capable of a high subsonic speed at low level.*

These particular MiG-27Ms are from 9 Squadron of the Indian Air Force, where they are known locally as Bahadur.

RIGHT: *The MiG-29 has been delivered to at least ten nations but has seen limited deliveries outside the ex-Warsaw Pact countries, with quantities operated by the North Koreans and Syria and a few being delivered to Iraq prior to the Gulf War. The Russians hope that further sales will provide more badly needed foreign currency.*

A further customer is the Indian Air Force, which took delivery of the first of 44 MiG-29s, including two two-seat trainers. Delivery of these commenced in December 1986 and they were for local assembly. A further batch of 20 was ordered in 1989.

This particular MiG-29 is flown by No. 28 Squadron.

INSERT RIGHT: *Preparing a Soviet-built, short-range AAM prior to it being loaded under the wing of an Indian Air Force MiG-29 from 28 Squadron, which is also fitted with the AA-10 "Alamo-A" medium range AAM.*

ABOVE: *The prototype of the MiG-29 "Fulcrum", which first flew on the 6th October 1977, was first noted on photographs taken by a US reconnaissance satellite of Ramenskoye flight test centre in the late '70s. The first public appearance of the MiG-29 in the West was when a detachment of six aircraft made a goodwill visit to Finland in July 1986.*

The MiG-29 is a single-seat counter-air fighter with an attack capability. This Soviet Air Force example is fitted with four AA-11 "Archer" short range AAMs and two AA-10 "Alamo A" medium range AAMs.

RIGHT: *A formation of four MiG-29As from 28 and 47 Squadrons of the Indian Air Force fly in formation. Two of the aircraft are painted in the air combat training colours.*

LEFT: *The Czechoslovak Air Force (as illustrated here) is equipped with 20 single-seat and four two-seat MiG-29s.*

The similarly-equipped East German Air Force has managed to acquire enough spares to keep its aircraft flying for several years following Reunification. This has given the NATO forces the opportunity physically to assess the aircraft, which has shown the MiG to be a potentially dangerous opponent, in the F-16 class.

ABOVE: *The latest of the Mikoyan and Gurevich family of fighters is the MiG-31 "Foxhound". Based on the MiG-25, the MiG-31 has two Perm D-30F6 turbofans which develop 20,950lb dry and 34,170lb with afterburner. It has a 23mm cannon visible in a bulge above the starboard main undercarriage bay. It also has recesses under the fuselage to accommodate four AA-9 "Amos" long range AAMs as well as carrying either AA-6 "Acrid" long range AAMs or AA-8 "Aphid" short range AAMs on pylons under the wings.*

RIGHT: *Visible are the recesses under the fuselage for the AA-9 "Amos" AAMs and the gun pod on the side of the fuselage. The air brakes can also be seen being deployed.*

ABOVE: *The Sukhoi Su-22 is a development of the Su-17, which was in turn a development of the Su-7. As a result the NATO name system has grouped them all together under the code "Fitter".*

The Su-7 was the standard strike fighter of the '60s and was a reliable aircraft, although somewhat lacking in capabilities. An Su-7 was modified to accept the variable geometry wing and made its first appearance to the West at the 1967 Aviation Day display at Domodedovo. This aircraft was given the NATO name of "Fitter-B". The performance of this aircraft proved to be a quantum leap over the Su-7 and it was placed straight into production as Su-17. This was designated as a ground support aircraft and as such could be fitted with a range of ordnance including gun pods, rockets and bombs (including nuclear). The Su-17 could carry twice the load of the Su-7 for a considerably greater distance. An export variant of the Su-17 was the Su-20 "Fitter-C", which was built to a lower standard.

A number of improvements have resulted in a second export variant known as the Su-22 "Fitter-F". While still intended primarily as an attack aircraft, the Su-22 is fitted with two 30mm cannon and can carry AA-2 "Atoll" AAMs, but is limited on range with internal fuel. It is probable that at least two of the six hardpoints would be used to carry fuel tanks.

Operators of the Su-22 include Afghanistan, Angola, Libya, Germany (ex-East German Air Force), Hungary (illustrated), Peru and Syria.

TOP RIGHT: *The Polish Air Force was the sole operator of the Su-17 "Fitter-K" outside the Soviet Union. These were later augmented by the Su-20, which was an export variant with reduced equipment. The Polish Air Force also has a number of the Su-22M4 "Fitter-Ks". This particular Su-22 is fitted with a pair of R-60 AAMs and four H-25MP anti-radiation AGMs.*

RIGHT: *The Su-24 "Fencer" is a two-seat variable geometry attack aircraft. This Su-24MR "Fencer-E" is the reconnaissance version and is from 11 Regiment of the Soviet Air Force currently based at Welzow, in what was East Germany.*

Following Reunification, plans were drawn up for the Soviet Forces to be withdrawn. However, due to the massive quantities of Soviet equipment throughout the now defunct Warsaw Pact countries, this is no easy matter.

The now disbanded 16th Air Army had well over 1,000 aircraft on strength and in time of tension the Soviets could deploy more than double this number to within 185km of the West German border, with another 1,600 within the next 185km. While the current numbers are nowhere near these, the problem of where all this equipment and manpower is to go is a major problem, and although the withdrawal programme is currently under way it will take some time to be completed.

RIGHT: *The Sukhoi Su-25 "Frogfoot" is the Soviet equivalent of the American A-10. Its role is ground attack, with a specialised function of "tank busting". It is fitted with eight underwing hardpoints to fit various weapons or stores. A further two pylons are fitted near the wing tips for air-to-air missiles.*

This Czechoslovak Air Force Sukhoi Su-25K is painted in appropriate markings especially for the Air Tournament International '92 airshow at A&AEE Boscombe Down. The Czech Air Force was the first recipient of the "Frogfoot A" outside the Soviet Air Force, and approximately 75 have been delivered.

BELOW: *The Bulgarian Air Force operates some 50 Sukhoi Su-25 "Frogfoot" ground attack aircraft, here seen fitted with a pair of the UB-16 rocket pods. In addition to the 250-plus of the Soviet Air Force and the 75 for the Czechoslovak Air Force, exports have also been made to North Korea. A few were also delivered to Iraq prior to the Gulf War.*

RIGHT: *The Sukhoi Su-27 "Flanker" first flew on 20th May 1977. It was designed as an air superiority fighter. The Su.27 is similar in shape and performance to the F-15 Eagle, although with a length of 70ft and a maximum take off weight of 66,138lb, it is larger and heavier. It has an impressive range in the region of close to 2,500 miles on maximum fuel. The improved, current version is powered by a pair of Lyulka AL-31F turbofans which give it a maximum speed of Mach 2.35 and a ceiling of 59,000 feet.*

A Naval variant of the Su-27 has been demonstrated aboard the Soviet carrier Admiral Nikolay Kuznetsov. These are launched under their own power, without the aid of a steam catapult. The carrier has a 12° ski jump which would permit an increased payload.

The Su-27 has been ordered by Afghanistan and China.

The large raised panel on the back of the Su-27 is the air brake, which has been deployed for landing.

ABOVE: *In June 1992 a Sukhoi Su-27P "Flanker" visited the UK to star in the Air Tournament International 92 airshow at A&AEE Boscombe Down. This aircraft was from the Flight Test Research Institute at Zhukovski, near Moscow.*

ABOVE: *The Pakistan Air Force operates aircraft from a number of sources. This mixed formation is led by an F-16A from 11 Squadron, with a Mirage 5PA on its wing. The nearest aircraft is a Shenyang F-6, which is a Chinese-built MiG-19. Both the F-6 and the Mirage are from the Combat Command School.*

During the late '50 the Chinese People's Republic imported a number of MiG-19s from the Soviet Union. When the two countries broke their relationship, China proceeded with a reverse engineering programme to build the MiG themselves. The first Chinese-built MiG-19 flew in December 1961 and production of several thousand followed.

A number of these have been supplied for export, and deliveries have been made to Albania, Bangladesh, Egypt, Ethiopia, North Korea, Pakistan, Somalia, Tanzania, Vietnam and Zambia.

RIGHT: *This formation of Pakistan Air Force aircraft is led by an F-7P of 20 Squadron with an F-6 of 15 Squadron, and nearest is the A-5C "Fantan-A" from 16 Squadron. Pakistan operated some 50 A-5Cs, which is a much modified MiG-19 designed and built in China. It has the air intakes moved to a position either side of the fuselage to accommodate a radar and is basically operated as an attack aircraft. In addition to bombs and rockets, the range of weapons that the A-5 is designed to carry can include the French R.550 Magic and AIM-9L Sidewinder, as well as the PL-5 and PL-7 AAMs. Pakistan is in the process of negotiating for up to 100 of the improved A-5Ms.*

ABOVE: *The Chinese have had success in exporting their aircraft as they are relatively inexpensive. In addition to the F-6s, the Pakistan Air Force operates a number of the CAC F-7P Skyguards in the air superiority role. This is a modified variant of the F-7M, the export version of the J-7 II directly based on the MiG-21, but including a few modifications including the fitting of an extra 30mm cannon. The F-7P also has increased range, with an improved WP-7BM engine, as well as an updated weapons control system and a wider weapons fit.*

RIGHT: *The Shenyang J-8 II "Finback B" is a major development from the original J-8 which first flew in 1969, and the J-8 is itself a descendant of the MiG-21. The J-8 II first flew on 12th June 1984 and is designed as a Mach-2.2, all-weather fighter/strike aircraft. Reported as being a 70 per cent redesign of the J-8 I, of which some 100 were delivered to the Chinese People's Liberation Army, this aircraft is now powered by a pair of WP-13A II turbojets. The nose intake has been moved and radar has been installed. The air intakes are now positioned on either side of the fuselage, between the cockpit and wing. Joint development with the US has resulted in Grumman designing and building the avionics suite which will include the fire control radar, inertial navigation system and head-up display. It has been designed to carry the PL-2A and PL-4 AAMs as well as being fitted with a 23mm twin-barrel cannon. It is planned that the J-8 II "Finback-B" will enter service with the Air Force of the People's Liberation Army in the mid 1990s.*

RIGHT: *The FT-7 is the training variant of the F-7, which again was evolved from the Soviet MiG-21. It is capable of carrying a range of weapons including the PL-2A AAM. As such it is used for weapon and gunnery training as well as for advanced pilot instruction.*

LEFT: *The Lockheed P-3 Orion may not be a fighter in the conventional sense of the word, but with a pair of Sidewinder AAMs it could surprise an attacking aircraft. The Orion was evolved from the Electra airliner and production has exceeded 500, with examples having been flown by the navies of Australia, Canada, Iran, Japan, Netherlands, New Zealand, Norway, Spain, as well as the USA.*

In addition to some highly sophisticated avionics for the ASW role, the Orion can carry a wide range of weaponry, including depth charges, torpedoes, mines, bombs, rockets, Harpoon ASM and even Sidewinders!

ABOVE: *The Hawker Siddeley Nimrod is another unlikely fighter as, like the Orion, its normal role is maritime patrol. It also has a similar evolution as it, too, was developed from an airliner: the de Havilland Comet.*

During the Falklands War, Nimrods were required to operate reconnaissance missions in the South Atlantic. To enable them to fly for the required extended periods they were fitted with refuelling probes so that they could be topped up with fuel from the Victor tankers. As the Nimrods were operating for considerable periods in hostile waters and well away from any possible air defence, it was decided

to fit Sidewinder AAMs under the wings. While the Nimrod might not have the look of a fighter, fitted with Sidewinders it would have been able to give a good account of itself in a one-to-one situation. Fortunately, such a confrontation did not occur.

ABOVE: *The EH.101 is the result of a joint agreement between Agusta of Italy and Westland in the UK to produce a successor to the Sea King, currently operated by both countries' navies. The design has included a utility (illustrated) and a civil variant, for which they see an eventual total requirement for some 750. The first of eight prototypes of the EH.101 made its maiden flight on 9th October 1987. Since then the further seven prototypes have been completed, including representatives of the proposed variants.*

The Utility EH.101 differs from the rest of the family in that it is fitted with a rear loading ramp. It is capable of lifting six tonnes or 35 combat troops. It is hoped that this variant will be ordered for the Royal Air Force to provide air mobility for the Army.

RIGHT: *Deck landing trials of the Italian prototype were satisfactorily carried out on the Italian Frigate Maestrale. The Italian Navy plans to acquire 38 EH.101 for the anti-submarine and anti-surface vessel role.*

In 1991 the British Government announced an order for 44 EH.101s for the Royal Navy, who will call it Merlin HAS.1. The Canadians have also selected the EH.101 as their Sea King replacement.

ABOVE: *The Puma was originally designed by Sud as a medium-sized tactical helicopter for the French Army. The prototype first flew on the 15th April 1965. In 1967 a joint Anglo/French agreement was signed for building the Puma, Gazelle and Lynx for both armed forces. The RAF took delivery of an initial order for 40 Pumas followed by an additional eight.*

The Westland Puma HC.1 of the RAF's 1563 Flight are tasked with a variety of duties due to the remoteness of the various positions in Belize. This Puma is on a replenishment run delivering various supplies, including fuel and a generator, to a mountain top Observation Post (OP) which overlooks Guatemala.

LEFT: *The Aerospatiale Puma has been developed progressively over the years and has now emerged as the Eurocopter Cougar. This is the military variant of the Super Puma. It is fitted with the higher powered Turbomeca Makila, which gives it an increased payload capacity. Typically, this means an increase in troop carrying capacity and increased range. The Cougar can carry 4.5 tonnes on its underslung hook. It is also capable of carrying a range of weapons*

The Puma/Super Puma/Cougar has seen a number of export successes to Brazil, China, Ivory Coast, Ethiopia, Gabon, Guinea, Indonesia, Lebanon, Malawi, Morocco, Portugal, Singapore, South Africa, Spain, Sweden, Switzerland and Venezuela. The Puma has also been built under licence in Romania, from where 15 were exported to Sudan.

This example of the AS.532SC Cougar is for the Brazilian Navy.

LEFT: *The Westland Lynx was the second of the helicopters covered by the Anglo-French joint development. The requirement was for a military helicopter with naval and ground-support variants. The design led by Westland resulted in the construction of 13 prototypes, of which the first took to the air on the 21st March 1971.*

The first production variant was the Lynx AH.1 for the British Army. This was a general purpose and utility helicopter which could be fitted with TOW for the anti-tank role, and 113 were built for the Army. An increase in engine power led to the AH.5, but this was almost immediately superseded by the AH.7, which included improved systems and changing the tail rotor direction. The AH.1s are being brought up to this standard.

A variant was planned for the RAF but these were delivered to the Army. This Lynx AH.1 is being refuelled and loaded with fresh TOW ATGWs during a replenishment while on operations in the Gulf during Desert Storm.

ABOVE: *The second variant of the Lynx was designed for naval use. Orders were placed for the Royal Navy and the French Navy. While both airframes are basically similar there are differences in the avionics fit.*

In Royal Navy service the role of the Lynx is to search, identify and attack enemy submarines or surface vessels from small ships. For this role the Lynx is armed with the Marconi Stingray lightweight torpedo or the BAe Sea Skua anti-ship missile.

The Royal Navy purchased 60 Westland Lynx HAS.2s and these have since been upgraded to HAS.3s. To these have been added a further batch of 30 Lynx HAS.3s.

The Royal Navy deployed the Lynx HAS.3 to the Gulf aboard a number of ships. These helicopters were from Nos 815 and 829 Squadrons and were subjected to a number of modifications. Illustrated here with HMS London *in the background, this Lynx HAS.3 can be seen fitted with an AN/ALQ-167 Yellow Veil pod designed to jam Exocet anti-ship*

missiles, and on top of the cabin are a pair of IR jammers.

During the Gulf War the RN Lynx were responsible for the sinking or disabling of 15 Iraqi patrol boats. The flights were based on HMS Battleaxe, Brazen, Cardiff, Gloucester, Jupiter, London (illustrated), Manchester and York, as well as a single Lynx aboard HMS Herald.

Recent orders have been built for the Portuguese Navy and the Korean Navy, adding to those already operated by Denmark, Germany, the Netherlands and Norway.

INSERT ABOVE: *RFA* Argus *provided the British forces with a casualty evacuation facility during the Gulf War. Almost as soon as she returned home* Argus *set the task of transporting helicopters for the Royal Marines deployed to Turkey, from where they were operated in support of the Kurds.*

Visible on deck of the RFA Argus *are Gazelles, Lynx and Sea Kings, the latter still having the black-and-white Allied identification marking applied during the Gulf War.*

LEFT: *Sixteen new Westland Lynx AH.9s together with a further eight converted from AH.1s will equip 9 Regiment of the AAC. Fitted with the new technology blade, the Lynx AH.9 has a 20 knot increase in cruising speed over previous marks.*

9 Regiment provides the Army Air Corp's contribution to the 24 Air Mobile Force (24AMF). This brigade is a light but well armed force which can be rapidly deployed to contain an advancing military force. Supported with RAF Chinooks and Pumas the entire force could be helilifted close to its objective. Vehicles in such an advance would be limited to Land Rovers and Light Strike Vehicles (LSVs).

RIGHT: *The Royal Navy Lynx has gradually taken over from the Westland Wasp in the roles of Anti-Submarine Warfare (ASW) and Anti-Surface Vessel warfare (ASV) from Royal Navy frigates and destroyers.*

The Sea Skua ASV missile is part of the weaponry of the Lynx and it became a very capable fighting system. The addition of a quantity of further electronic kit during the Armilla patrols and Gulf War, has increased the crews' workload close to the limit. As a result a further variant – the HAS.8 – is currently being introduced in phased modification. It will include a new gearbox and the fitting of composite rotor blades plus a reversal of the tail rotor direction to reduce the noise factor; a new attack system, based on that already used by the Dutch Lynx, whereby information from the various sensors is input into a central computer and presented on a screen to the crew (currently each piece of information is plotted manually onto a board); secure communications, and finally the fitting of GEC Sea Owl to provide a passive ship identification.

A further role for which the Lynx is used is that of communications and observation. HMS Endurance provided a platform for Antarctic survey for many years, but this ship has now retired and was replaced in 1990 by the HMS Polar Circle. She is equipped with the Lynx with high visibility markings together with a pod which contains a stabilised TV system.

LEFT: *The Gazelle is the third of the helicopters covered under the Anglo-French agreement. Designed by Sud, the prototype SA.340 Gazelle first flew on the 7th April 1967. It was conceived as a five-seat, all purpose light helicopter and is operated by all three of the British armed forces.*

It has replaced the Sioux in Army Air Corps service and is operated in a number of roles, of which training and battlefield observation are probably the greatest. The latter can be in conjunction with the TOW armed Lynx in the ATGW role. The Gazelle can also be used as an air ambulance. In the past it has been fitted with a machine gun and SNEB rocket pods for the attack role and can also be fitted with a GPMG behind the pilot. A further use in liaison/communications is a role for which it is well suited.

Illustrated is one of the 99 Gazelle AH.1s of the AAC. This Gazelle is operated by 7 Flight, which is stationed at RAF Gatow in Berlin and can be seen flying along what was the border fence with East Germany, on a recce patrol.

RIGHT: *This Gazelle AH.1 can be seen at Kuwait International Airport just after the end of the Gulf War. It is being used here in the communication role but spent much of the war flying scout missions for the Lynx.*

BELOW: *The Royal Navy took delivery of 30 Gazelle HT.2s for basic helicopter training. They are nearly all flown by 705 Squadron at RNAS Culdrose, where student pilots have already been given some fixed wing training and are introduced to the helicopter for their basic flying training. On successfully completing the course the student will then proceed to 706 and 810 Squadrons for their advanced flying training on the Sea King.*

705 Squadron also provides the crew and helicopters for the Royal Navy Sharks display team. The Sharks comprise a volunteer group of individuals who rehearse and run the team in their spare time, presenting a highly professional and polished display at numerous events throughout the year.

LEFT: *Aerospatiale continue to manufacture the Gazelle and have exported it widely. Typical is this SA.342L Gazelle from 6 Close Support Squadron, which is one of 12 operated by the Qatar Emiri Air Force. It is flown in the attack role, for which it is equipped with the Euromissile HOT ATGW missile. They are flying over a platoon of Qatar Emiri Army AMX-30 main battle tanks. A further two SA.342G Gazelles are operated in the communication role as well as in support of the police.*

BELOW: *The French Army have approximately 350 Gazelles, which they operate as replacements for the Alouette II. 188 of the Gazelles are of the SA.341M version, which is armed with the Euromissile HOT ATGW.*

ABOVE: *This AAC Gazelle AH.1 is based at the British Army Training Unit Suffield (BATUS) training ground in Canada. It is seen here operating in the classic observation role, where it is hidden behind some ground cover but is able to see the battlefield. From here information could be radioed or flown back to commanders, or to direct the TOW armed Lynx.*

RIGHT: *The Royal Air Force operates the Gazelle HT.3 specifically for the basic helicopter training role, although a few additional Gazelle HCC.4s are used as VIP transports. A number of the Army AH.1s are also used for training purposes at AAC Middle Wallop.*

Breaking formation is an RAF Gazelle HT.3 of 2 FTS based at RAF Shawbury.

LEFT: *The origins of the Westland Wessex stem from a 1951 US Navy requirement for an anti-submarine helicopter. Sikorsky designed and built the S-58 to meet this requirement and it took to the air for the first time on the 8th March 1954. The S-58 was widely used by the US armed forces and was exported to a number of countries.*

A British requirement for such a helicopter resulted in Westland entering into a licence production agreement. This resulted in orders for the Royal Navy for ASW duties and later commando transport. The Wessex HC.2 was ordered for the RAF for the medium transport role and the first delivery was made in 1963. It currently remains in service with 72 and 60 Squadrons as well as 22 Squadron, whose bright yellow helicopters share the Search And Rescue (SAR) duties around the UK with 202 Squadron's Sea Kings.

BELOW: *The Westland Wasp first flew on the 28th October 1962 as the new Royal Navy anti-submarine helicopter. A number were later exported to various countries including Brazil, Netherlands, and South Africa.*

Although retired from Royal Navy service the Wasp is still flown by the Royal New Zealand Navy.

RIGHT: *The Westland Scout was conceived from the Saunders Roe P.531 design which first flew on the 20th July 1958. Some 120 were ordered for the Army Air Corps as a five-seat general purpose helicopter. It has seen extensive service with the AAC in numerous locations throughout the world. It has also been used in a wide variety of roles. These include attack, for which the SS11 guided anti-tank missile was fitted and air ambulance, for which two stretchers could be carried internally plus a further two in external panniers. It has an underslung load lifting capability although the weight carried is somewhat limited. It is still used as a troop transport. The Scout AH.1 has been largely replaced by the Lynx but it is still popular and remains in reasonable numbers.*

LEFT: *The Westland Sea King is the result of a licence agreement with Sikorsky made in 1959. Adapted to include British engines and equipment, the Royal Navy Sea King was required to replace the Wessex in the anti-submarine warfare (ASW) role. The first of 56 HAS.1s took to the air on 7th May 1969.*

Further development of the Sea King resulted in the HAS.2, of which 21 were built for the RN and in addition 47 were converted from HAS.1s and designated HAS.2A.

To assist in the development of the ASW avionics, several Sea Kings were purchased for the RAE and painted in their distinctive "Raspberry Ripple" colour scheme. An RAF Wessex HC.2 formates behind.

Westland have been quite successful with export of the Sea King, deliveries having been made to Australia, Belgium, Egypt, India, Norway (11) Pakistan and Germany.

RIGHT: *The Westland Sea King HC.4 is a development of the exported Westland Commando. It retains the folding rotors and tail of the Sea King but with the fixed undercarriage of the Commando. The Sea King HC.4 can carry 28 fully equipped troops or 8,000lbs of freight internally or underslung. A total of 37 HC.4s were ordered for the RN. They have seen active service during the Falklands War and are regularly exercised in the Arctic conditions of northern Norway, as well as in much warmer areas.*

During the Gulf War 846 Squadron was deployed aboard RFA Fort Grange and RFA Argus. The RFA Fort Grange is a Fleet Replenishment Ship containing all types of ship's stores. Two Sea Kings were kept aboard to provide the "VertRep" – the transferring of the stores to ships at sea by helicopter. The rest of 846's complement of Sea Kings were aboard the RFA Argus.

In peacetime the RFA Argus is a helicopter training ship, but during the Gulf War she became a Primary Casualty Receiving Ship. One of the lessons from the Falklands War was that the distance between the battle and the hospital ship was too great. Below decks RFA Argus has three hangars. One was filled with a system of portakabins to provide a hospital facility. The role of the ship was to be as close as possible to the combat with the helicopters flying to recover the casualties and transport them to the ship for treatment.

ABOVE: *The Westland Sea King HAR.3 is the Royal Air Force's main SAR helicopter, which it operates in conjunction with the Wessex HC.2.*

ABOVE: *The Royal Navy deployed 845 Sqn Sea Kings along with the newly formed 848 Sqn to the Gulf aboard the new* Atlantic Conveyor. *Once in Saudi Arabia the Sea King HC.4s were deployed in support of 1 (BR) Armoured Division. Affectionately known as the "Junglies" due to their Commando role, the HC.4s were painted pink and it was a long time before they saw trees again.*

RIGHT: *Night Vision Goggles (NVG) were developed to enable aircrew to fly at night in near blackout conditions. The NVG are a light intensifier, requiring a small amount of ambient light from the moon to amplify and produce an image that the pilot can recognise and fly by. In the Gulf many aircrew were equipped with NVG, which enabled them to fly night missions.*

RIGHT: *The Westland Sea King HC.4s of all three squadrons were armed with GPMGs for self protection, even those of 846 employed in the casevac role. The function of RFA* Argus *required her to be close to trouble, and as such it was felt that the Red Cross symbol alone would be unlikely to provide sufficient protection. As a result the ship was also fitted with guns and missiles for her self defence.*

BOTTOM RIGHT: *The Westland Sea King AEW.2 was a priority product of the Falklands War when it was discovered that the lack of an Airborne Early Radar (AEW) was to cause avoidable losses. The highly successful attacks by the Argentinian Super Etendards equipped with the Exocet ASM caused considerable damage. Had there been AEW cover these would have been detected early enough and dealt with. The reason for there not being an AEW aircraft available was that the previous type – the Fairey Gannet AEW.3 – was scrapped with the disposal of the last conventional carrier. It was not envisaged that the new generation of Sea Harrier-equipped carriers would operate outside an area where land based AEW would be available. The Falklands brought this omission forcefully home. The Westland answer was to fit the Searchwater radar onto a HAS.2A in an inflatable radome.*

This Sea King AEW.2 is from "B" Flight of 849 Squadron based on HMS Ark Royal.

LEFT: *Further developments have been incorporated into 56 existing Sea King HAS.2/2A airframes and an additional order placed for 30 new Sea Kings, all of which are designated HAS.5. The pair of Gnome H.1400-1 turboshaft engines are now rated 1,660shp and maximum take off weight increased to 21,000lb compared with 1,500shp and 20,500lb on the HAS.1. The HAS.5 is equipped with the Sea Search radar. For underwater detection it is equipped with passive sonobuoys and dipping sonar, which integrate into a single display system. It is also fitted with an ESM system.*

The next generation of Sea King is the HAS.6, for which four new helicopters were ordered in 1987. This version includes an improved sonar as well as an improved secure communications system. The existing HAS.5 airframes are gradually being modified up to this state.

ABOVE: *The Westland Commando is a development of the Sea King basic airframe optimised for troop carrying.*

The Qatar Emiri Air Force (illustrated) operate eight Commando 3s with No. 8 (Anti-Surface Vessel) Squadron and can be fitted with the Exocet ASM. No. 9 Squadron is equipped with three Commando 2As, with which it undertakes a variety of missions including assault, plus a further Commando 2C which has a VIP interior.

A further customer for the Commando was Egypt, which took delivery of 28 for VIP and ECM duties.

LEFT: *The Boeing Vertol Model 114 was designed as a battlefield mobility helicopter for the US Army. It was capable of carrying 16,000lbs internally or 4,000lbs underslung. It also had to accommodate 40 troops with full equipment, have a rear loading ramp and be able to airlift any component of the Pershing missile system. An initial order was placed for five YHC-1Bs (re-designated YHC-1A) in June 1959, and the first hover was made on 21st September 1961. First production deliveries to the US Army, designated CH-47A, did not commence until December 1972, by which time the helicopter had been named Chinook.*

The Chinook proved to be a successful helicopter in Vietnam - not only for troop and supply missions but also for rescue and the recovery of crashed aircraft. This CH-47D Chinook is at Kuwait International Airport at the end of the Gulf War, with the oil wells burning in the background. The front window has been removed to enable a machine gun to be fitted for self defence.

A number of countries ordered the Chinook, including Argentina, Australia, Canada, Greece, Singapore, Spain, Thailand and Turkey.

LEFT: *Meridionali of Italy obtained a licence agreement from Boeing in which it could market the Chinook in the Middle East, resulting it deliveries to Egypt, Iran, Libya, Morocco as well as this example for the Italian Army for which it built 28.*

Additional licence production is carried out by Kawasaki for the Japanese Army and Air Self Defence Force, for which a requirement of 54 exists.

RIGHT: *RAF Chinook crews take a break during a lull in the intensive flying in the Gulf. The sand proved to be a troublesome environment for all helicopters in the Gulf, especially the Chinooks, with their massive downwash, this despite the fitting of large sand filters on the engines. As in the Falklands, the Chinook was found to be vital for moving troops or supplies quickly.*

LEFT: *The British Government ordered 33 Chinooks in 1978 to satisfy an RAF heavy lift requirement. Unfortunately, three were lost in the South Atlantic when the* Atlantic Conveyor *was hit by an Exocet missile. However, a further order was placed for eight as replacements. This Chinook HC.1 of 240 OCU is carrying two fuel cells and a quantity of ammunition as an underslung load from its three hooks.*

RIGHT: *The Boeing MH-47E Chinook has been specifically developed to meet the demanding need of the US Army's 160th Special Operations Aviation Regiment. The MH-47E is a remanufactured CH-47C which is equipped with highly advanced avionics as well as extended range which can be further extended by aerial refuelling. It also has increased power which, when combined, enable it to complete deep penetration missions in poor weather condition by day or night and at very low level with greatly reduced workload on the pilot. The US Army has a current requirement for 51 MH-47Es.*

RIGHT: *The S-65/H-53 was designed to meet the US Navy and US Marine Corps requirement for a heavy lift helicopter capable of loading vehicles or freight through a rear ramp. The programme was assisted by the inclusion of the already proven CH-54 Tahre rotors and transmission. In 1962 an order was placed for two prototypes, the first of which made its maiden flight on the 14th October 1964. After a successful evaluation deliveries commenced to units in September 1966, and within a few months they were deployed to Vietnam.*

The CH-53 has a range of just over 250 miles and the ability to operate day or night and in poor weather. It can carry 37 fully armed troops or a payload of around 30,000lbs.

The CH-53 has been ordered by the USAF, USN and USMC for a variety of roles, including SAR, assault and minesweeping.

The need to deploy fighters and strike aircraft to the Gulf quickly was achieved with aerial refuelling, but this was impossible for the helicopters. While a number were accommodated in aircraft carriers and assault ships, large numbers were flown over inside giant C-5 Galaxy or C-141 Starlifters. Designed for naval operations, the CH-53 is capable of being folded to reduce its footprint. While the UH-1, AH-1 and AH-64 helicopters could be simply loaded into the aircraft, the larger CH-53 still required the rotor head and gearbox to be removed prior to loading.

ABOVE: *The German Army had a requirement for a heavy lift helicopter so competitive trials were held to compare the CH-47 Chinook with the CH-53. The result was that the German Government ordered 133 licence-built examples of the CH-53 in 1966, but this was subsequently cut to 110 in 1972 due to rising costs.*

Further examples of the S-65/H-53 were ordered by Austria and Israel.

RIGHT: *The USAF special forces have been using the HH-53 for a number of special operations over the years. The introduction of the MH-53H Pave Low II and the new MH-53J Pave Low has provided them with a dedicated helicopter with a highly sophisticated avionics suite.*

LEFT: *During Desert Storm a large number of CH-53s were deployed to the Gulf. This US Marine Corps (USMC) CH-53 of HMH-466 hovers while a British Army Ferret Scout Car is prepared for airlift during joint operations in the Gulf War. A machine gun is fitted where the window has been removed.*

RIGHT: *The Boeing Vertol CH-46 Sea Knight is the US Marine Corps utility helicopter. It flew in prototype form on 22nd April 1958. Conceived as a private venture, the testing and development, together with a demonstration tour, provoked a great deal of interest. A civil variant was built as the Model 107.*

The US Marine Corps became interested in 1961 and the CH-46 entered production. A total of 624 Sea Knights were delivered to the US Navy and Marine Corps over the period 1964-71. In the mid '70s a programme commenced to upgrade most of the fleet up to CH-47E standard, which included a higher powered engine and glassfibre rotor blades as well as avionics and hydraulics upgrades.

The USN and USMC use the CH-46/UH-46 for a variety of roles, including vertical replenishment (vertrep) of stores from ship to ship, and troop transport.

A number of the CH-46 Sea Knights were deployed to the Gulf for Desert Storm. Al Jubail was a central point for large numbers of helicopters arriving in the Gulf, and later for the departure. Ten squadrons of CH-46E Sea Knights were deployed for Desert Storm, where they were flown by the USMC in the assault helicopter role.

ABOVE: *The McDonnell Douglas AH-64A Apache is designed to meet the US Army requirement for an advanced attack helicopter. It had to be capable of flying an anti-tank role in most weather conditions, by day or night. For this role it is highly manoeuvrable and has good acceleration. It is equipped with 70mm rockets and/or up to 16 of the laser guided Hellfire anti-tank guided missiles in addition to the 30mm gun fitted under the nose.*

The US Army plans to have 40 Apache units for which they have ordered 807 aircraft. Each Apache Battalion is equipped with 18 AH-64s and is supported by 13 OH-58 Kiowa scouts and three UH-60s.

Prior to Desert Shield the Apache had received a considerable amount of bad publicity regarding its cost and serviceability record. It was thought that operating in a very hot and sandy environment would create even worse readiness rates. Instead, the AH-64 Apache exceeded all other helicopters in the Gulf and was well above the US Army standard of 75 per cent, achieving in excess of 90 per cent.

Exports include 12 to Saudi, 24 to Egypt, 18 for Israel, 20 for UAE, 12 for Greece, 37 for Korea and 30 for Kuwait.

LEFT: *Boeing Vertol granted a licence to Japan to build a quantity of CH-46s for their own defence force. They were built by Kawasaki and known as the Kv.107.*

Further operators of variants of the CH-46 include Canada (CH-113 Labrador) and Sweden (HKP-4).

LEFT: *The AH-64 Apache is seen firing its 70mm rockets. Alternatively, it is capable of carrying 16 Hellfire AGM or four Stinger AAMs in addition to the 1,200 rounds of ammunition for its M230 Chain Gun. Weapon options include Maverick AGM and various AAMs including Sidewinder and Mistral.*

TV coverage of Desert Storm allowed actual combat film to be seen, showing the effectiveness of the complete system in action. The crews watching the screens in their cockpit, which give them enhanced vision of targets at night, picking the targets and then destroying them gave the impression of a computer game rather than real warfare. Such was the effectiveness of the imagery and the perceived threat that on some attacks Iraqi soldiers could be seen abandoning their vehicles as soon as they were aware that the helicopters were attacking. The Iraqis nicknamed the Apache "Black Death".

Four prototypes of the Longbow Apache are being used to develop the next generation of the AH-64. Among the system enhancements is the Mast Mounted Sight (MMS). It is planned that 227 of the AH-64As will be configured to the AH-64D Longbow Apache.

LEFT: *The Bell AH-1 HueyCobra commenced as a company funded project in the early '60s to build a helicopter for armed missions. The initial designs were based on the B.47 Sioux, but this was soon dropped in favour of the UH-1 Iroquois. About this time the US Army realised that events in Vietnam required such a helicopter. A prototype flew on 7th September 1965. Such was its success that the US Army ordered two pre-production prototypes within a few days and an initial batch of 110 Hueys the following April. By January the US Army had ordered 1,008.*

This AH-1G HueyCobra is from the 1/224th Attack Helicopter Battalion of the 29th Aviation Brigade, which is part of Maryland's Army National Guard. It is based at Weide Army Airfield on the edge of Aberdeen Proving Ground.

BELOW: *The USMC Hueys flew in various colour schemes during Desert Storm in the Gulf. While some were operated in their normal grey scheme, these AH-1Ws of HMLA-369 were sprayed a light sand colour over this. Others were completely sprayed in sand and brown.*

ABOVE: *Exports include Israel, which is currently planning to upgrade her AH-1S Cobras. This will provide a new night target information system and the ability to launch Hellfire missiles.*

The Jordanian Air Force (illustrated) has 24 TOW-equipped AH-1S Cobras which were received in 1985 and are operated by Nos 10 and 12 Squadrons.

The Pakistan Army have 20 AH-1S Cobras, 10 delivered in '84 and a further 10 in '86, with Bell 206s as scouts. A further 10 AH-1Fs were offered to meet a requirement, but Congress subsequently suspended military assistance because of Pakistan's suspected nuclear weapons development. The Spanish Navy has eight AH-1Gs for the anti-shipping role.

RIGHT: *The Bell AH-1W SuperCobra is the latest variant for the US Marine Corps. Of this model 127 are currently being delivered, with a requirement for a further 79. Nicknamed the "Whiskey Cobra", this attack helicopter can carry up to eight Hellfire or TOW II missiles plus two AIM-9L Sidewinders and a pair of 70mm rocket launchers. It is also fitted with a three-barrelled 20mm M197 cannon.*

LEFT: *The Sikorsky UH-60 Blackhawk was designed to meet the US Army Utility Tactical Transport Aircraft System (UTTAS) requirement to replace the UH-1s. In competition with Boeing's UH-61, the US Army ordered three flying prototypes of each for evaluation. The UH-60 was the first to fly on the 17th October 1974. Fourteen months later the UH-60 was selected and production commenced on a planned requirement of 1,107.*

The Blackhawk can carry 11 troops in addition to its crew of three. An external hook enables it to carry underslung loads. During the Gulf War the UH-60A was widely used and fitted with 7.62mm M-60 machine guns mounted in the doorways.

RIGHT: *The Sikorsky SH-60 Seahawk is the US Navy derivative of the Army Blackhawk. It operates as three variants within the US Navy. The SH-60B is the air component of the Light Airborne Multipurpose System (LAMPS) Mk.III weapon system, replacing the Kaman Seasprite. Apart from delivering weapons it can act as a platform for battle group radar and electronic warfare support.*

The SH-60F Ocean Hawk is designed as a replacement for the SH-3H Sea King for the ASW and ASV roles, for which it has improved capabilities.

The third variant is the HH-60H Seahawk, and this is designed for strike rescue and Naval special warfare support, for which it is completely night vision capable.

This SH-60B Seahawk is operated by HSL-42.

ABOVE: *Westland have assembled a prototype of the Sikorsky Blackhawk, designated WS-70. The two companies agreed to licence production in the UK of this variant, which they hope will be accepted for the British services. Westland have added the role of assault helicopter to the Blackhawk's already effective capability by the fitting of a pair of pylons to which a range of weapons can be attached, including rockets, guns and cannon.*

LEFT: *The Westland Blackhawk can be fitted with a range of weaponry which includes four 2.75 inch rocket pods.*

RIGHT: *One of the vital roles of the Sikorsky UH-60 Blackhawk is that of battlefield casualty evacuation (CASEVAC). For this role the UH-60 of 421st Aviation Battalion can be fitted with a stanchion in the cab, on which are four litters. Each litter tilts down to assist with the loading and then the whole assembly can be swivelled through 90°. This still leaves room for seven troop seats.*

BELOW: *The S-70A-1L Desert Hawk is a specially-equipped variant of the Blackhawk configured to carry out medical evacuation missions. It is fitted with external hoists and provision for six litters. In addition it has a high intensity searchlight with infrared filters, air conditioning and advanced avionics and communications systems.*

The Royal Saudi Land Forces Army Aviation Command is taking delivery of eight of this variant with a requirement for a further eight. Other exports include 39 S-70A-9s for the RAAF and 16 S-70B-2 Seahawks for their Navy, which were assembled in Australia. These incorporate a number of locally manufactured components and the fitting of the more powerful T700-GE-701A1 engines. Deliveries are being made to Japan and Spain with further orders received from Greece.

LEFT: *The Bell OH-58 Kiowa was announced as the winner of a further US Army requirement for a light observation helicopter following problems with previous LOH orders. The OH-58A is basically similar to the Model 206A Jet Ranger, which first flew on the 10th January 1966. The first delivery to the Army of 2,200 OH-58s began on 23rd May 1969. The role of this helicopter was to be casualty evacuation, close support, observation, photo-reconnaissance, and light transport.*

This OH-58 is refuelling at a field replenishment point. It is being flown with the AH-64A Apache as a scout. In this role it spots the enemy armour for the Apache.

ABOVE: *The Sikorsky Sea King was originally designated HSS-1 and was designed as an ASW hunter/killer helicopter. Developments in the various sensors, equipment and avionics dictated a cabin area much larger than that of the S-58 which it was to replace. In 1957 an order was placed for seven test aircraft and the first took to the air on 11th March 1959. Deliveries commenced two years later.*

Illustrated is one of the Sikorsky SH-3H Sea Kings of HS-11 "Dragonslayers", searching ahead of USS America during a sub-hunting mission. During the launch and recovery sequences on the carrier a Sea King also flies in the close vicinity as crash guard, ready to provide immediate assistance in the event of an incident.

RIGHT: *The Bell OH-58D Kiowa is based on the OH-58A airframe but is fitted with an advanced Mast Mounted Sight (MMS) as part of the US Army helicopter improvement programme. Designed and built by McDonnell Douglas, the MMS is a fully integrated, multi-sensor, electro-optical system for surveillance and detection. It uses TV and infrared to assist the crew in acquiring targets. The OH-58D Kiowa is armed with a pair of rocket pods.*

LEFT: *The Bell UH-1D/H (Model 205) is developed from the Bell UH-1A/B (Model 204), which first flew on 22nd October 1956. It was initially known as the H-40, the HU-1 (from where the name "Huey" originated) then later became the UH-1. The first YUH-1D flew on 16th August 1961 and was basically a stretched fuselage now capable of carrying 14 troops compared with seven previously. The UH-1D/H became the workhorse of Vietnam. It has sold widely throughout the world and there are numerous local production agreements.*

The 29th Aviation Brigade is made up of a Company of the UH-1H Hueys in addition to Cobras and Kiowas. They will gradually be augmented with the UH-60A Blackhawk, deliveries of which have now commenced.

The UH-1 is used as a primary, instrument and navigation trainer for entry-level US Army pilots. Currently costing some $600 per hour, the US Army is looking at leasing 180 off-the-shelf helicopters as a cheaper option now that the UH-1 is nearing the end of its useful life.

RIGHT: *The UH-1 has provided the US Army with the backbone of its assault helicopter force for many years. It is hardly surprising that significant numbers of UH-1s were deployed to the Gulf and used by the US Army and Marine Corps. Many were flown out by the constant stream of C-5s and C-141s which operated a shuttle service from the USA and other locations. These USMC UH-1s and AH-1s are at Al Jubail at the end of the war, awaiting shipment back home.*

LEFT: *A UH-1 from a previous conflict is this ex-Argentinian Army Iroquois. This helicopter was operated by the Argentine Army, which had occupied the Falkland Islands by force in 1982. At the end of Operation Corporate, as this conflict was named, this UH-1 was discovered to be serviceable and had not suffered damage, unlike most of the others on the Islands. With a shortage of helicopters available to the British Forces, and the hostile countryside, the UH-1 was put to good use, with a total of 15 hours being clocked up.*

Some while later the UH-1 was brought back to the UK as part of the spoils of war. Flt Lt Rob Tierney and his team managed to gain the support of numerous organisations and manufacturers to assist in restoring the UH-1 to a fully airworthy condition. Eventually G-HUEY, as she was now officially registered, was sold by the RAF to the Royal Air Force Benevolent Fund for a nominal one pound. She was displayed at numerous airshows to raise money for the Fund and has since been sold.

Left: *The Bell UH-1 was built under licence in Italy by Agusta in various models, including the AB.204, AB.205, AB.212, as well as the AB.206 Jet Ranger. Apart from production for the Italian military and civilian requirements Agusta markets the range throughout Europe and the Middle East. Typical customers are Iran, Spain, Turkey and Saudi Arabia. A further customer, where the AB.204B is designated Hkp-3, is the Swedish military, operated by their Navy and Army (as illustrated).*

Below: A total of 45 Bell 214STs were ordered by the Iraqi Ministry of Transportation for civil operations, but at least one found its way into military service. Found abandoned at Kuwait International Airport at the end of the war by members of the USMC, this surviving helicopter found itself being returned to the USA as war booty.

Above: The threat by Saddam Hussain to use chemical weapons was taken very seriously by the Allied forces, and as a result a major support force in the form of extensive medical facilities was established early on in the deployment phase, with further facilities prepared in the home countries. Vital links in the chain were the Casevac helicopters such as these UH-1s, which would have been required to fly into the battle zone to recover those injured and feed them into the medical chain.

Right: The Bell UH-1 has seen wide use around the world. This UH-1H is from 3 Squadron of the Royal New Zealand Air Force.

LEFT: *Designed by Hughes for the US Army light helicopter requirement, an initial order was placed for four prototypes. Designated OH-6, the helicopter first flew on 27th February 1963. An order for the production of 714 was placed for the OH-6 and this was increased to 1,434. Hughes developed a civilian and an export series which was designated Model 500. This was the beginning of a series of helicopters with variations of engine and equipment. Depending on the model a wide range of weapons can be fitted, including TOW, Hellfire and Stinger missiles as well as cannon. Licence production agreements were established with a number of countries including Argentina, Italy and Japan (illustrated).*

The McDonnell Douglas 500/OH-6 has seen wide use, with substantial deliveries to the US Army. Export of a number of variants has also been made to the armed forces of many countries, including Colombia, Denmark, El Salvador, Finland, Haiti, Israel, Jordan, Kenya, Mexico, Philippines, Spain and South Korea.

ABOVE: *The A.129 Mangusta is a light anti-tank, attack and advanced scout helicopter designed by Agusta to incorporate mission flexibility. It made its official first flight on 15th September 1983. It can carry eight TOW2A missiles or four 81mm rocket pods in addition to a 12.7mm gun turret. The Italian Army plans to receive 30 of the scout-configured Agusta A.129 Mangusta in addition to 60 of the anti-tank version.*

RIGHT: *The Harbin Z9 is the Chinese licence-built version of the SA.365N Dauphin II. The Z9 is capable of a wide variety of roles, including communications, with 10 passengers, as an air ambulance and troop carrier. A variant has also been developed for the anti-tank role, equipped with the Hongjian missile. The agreement is for an initial batch of 50 Z9s, which will be divided between civilian and military duties.*

LEFT: *This LHX is the Boeing/ Sikorsky proposal for the next generation of light helicopter for the US Army to replace the AH-1, OH-6 and OH-58. The planned requirement is approaching 3,000 helicopters. The project is currently proceeding through the demonstration/validation prototyping phase.*

ABOVE: *The Mil Mi.8 "Hip-A" was first shown to the public at the 1961 Aviation Day display at Tushino. It is a medium transport helicopter, of which there are a number of civil and military variants.*

The "Hip-C" variant is the standard example for the Soviet armed forces for tactical transport, and some 1,500 have been built. It has racks on either side of the fuselage onto which four pods can be attached, containing 128 x 57mm rockets.

This Mil.8 is operated by the Polish Army Aviation.

RIGHT: *A Mil Mi.8 painted in desert camouflage, in storage at a Hungarian overhaul facility for an embargoed Middle East customer.*

LEFT: *The Mil Mi.2 "Hoplite" is a twin turbo-engine powered development from the Mi.1 "Hare". The 40 per cent additional power more than doubles the payload of the Mi.2. Although it was designed in the Soviet Union the Mi.2 was unique in that the whole of production for the Soviets and Warsaw Pact countries was carried out by PZL Swidnik of Poland.*

This Hungarian Mi.2 is from the Asboth Oszkar Helicopter Regiment, which is based at Borgond.

RIGHT: *The Mi-8 has a number of specialised sub-variants for specialist roles, such as the "Hip-G" with rearward-facing airborne communications, "Hip-J" for ECM and "Hip-K" for communications jamming.*

This Mil Mi.8S "Hip C" is from the Hungarian Dragon training squadron.

ABOVE: *The Mil Mi.17 "Hip-H" was first displayed at the 1981 Paris Air Show. It was developed in parallel with the Mi.14 "Haze", which is a maritime variant with a boat hull on the bottom of the fuselage.*

This Soviet Mi.17 is fitted with the S-21 rocket pod as well as a flare dispenser.

LEFT: *The Mil-17 "Hip-H" is the Mi-8 fitted with the uprated power plant used on the Mi14 and 24.*

This Indian Air Force Mi.17 from No. 129 Squadron is on a training sortie from its base near Delhi. It is armed with six of the UB-16 rocket pods.

LEFT: The Mil Mi.28 "Havoc" is an attack helicopter still in development, although it first flew on 10th November 1982. The distinctive nose consists of a radome, beneath which are a sight and a laser designator. It is fitted with a pair of UV-20 pods which have a capacity of 20 2.24in S5 or 3.15 S8 rockets, plus eight AT-6 "Spiral" ATM canisters at each tip station. It is likely that production Mi.28s will be fitted with a higher powered cannon.

ABOVE: The Mil Mi.24 "Hind" probably originally flew in 1970. It was conceived in the early '60s by Mikhail Mil, about the same time as the Bell AH-1 Huey. Based on the central core of the Mi.8, the Mi.24 initially took the rotor, power plant and dynamic systems, although they were all later upgraded.

Designed as a helicopter gunship, the Mi.24 also has the capability of carrying eight combat-equipped troops.

This Soviet Forces Mi.24 It is fitted with a UV-20 57mm rocket pod, of which four can be fitted. The stub wing endplate also acts as a missile pylon for the AT-6 "Spiral" ATGW.

BELOW: The Mil Mi.35 "Hind E & F" is the export variant of the Mi.24. Along with the Mi.25, production of this family of helicopters is estimated to have exceeded 2,500.

This pair of Indian Air Force Mi.35s from No. 104 Helicopter Flight are fitted with flare dispensers; the thimble-shaped object above them is an infra-red emitter to distract heat-seeking missiles.

RIGHT: Besides the role of helicopter gunship, the Mi.24 is thought to have the role of escort to the troop-carrying Mi.8 and Mi.17. It is also considered capable of attacking and destroying opposition helicopters in an air-to-air scenario.

This line up of six Mi.24s is from the Hungarian Bakony Attack Regiment.

LEFT: *The desire of the Polish Government to reduce their dependence on Soviet hardware for their armed services and develop their own aircraft industry has resulted in the W-3. Designed and built by PZL Swidnik, it is named Sokol. It has been designed as a multi-purpose helicopter aimed at the civil as well as the military market. The prototype first flew on the 16th November 1979.*

Two military variants of the W-3 Sokol have emerged. The first is the Anakonda, which is entering service with the Polish Naval Aviation in the SAR role. A total of 12 helicopters are planned to replace the Mil Mi.14PS "Haze-C".

RIGHT: *The second variant of the W-3 Sokol that PZL have recently produced in prototype form is of a new, armed utility helicopter named the Salamanda. It is intended for the Polish Army and will incorporate a mission equipment package based on the Mil Mi.24 Hind. It is armed with a twin GSh-23 cannon plus stub wing mounted AT-6 Spiral missiles and/or 80mm rocket pods.*

BELOW RIGHT: *The Alouette III is an enlarged development of the Alouette II with an increased cabin capacity. By replacing the IIC-6 with the increased power of the Artouste IIIB, the Alouette III was significantly improved. The prototype made its first flight on 28th February 1959 and rapidly proved itself, establishing a number of high altitude records.*

Besides French production of some 1,500, licence production by HAL has produced some 200 helicopters for the Indian Army, while a further agreements with Switzerland and ICA-Brassov in Romania extended production even further. Export has been extensive, nearly 50 countries having operated new or refurbished Alouette IIIs in a military role.

The Royal Netherlands Air Force operates a number of the Alouette IIIs for SAR and Army support, although in a partial replacement it plans to lease a quantity of attack helicopters in 1994.

LEFT: *The Aerospatiale SA-321 Super Frelon was developed with assistance from Sikorsky, and it took to the air for the first time on 7th December 1962. It was designed as a large utility helicopter but entered production for the ASW role. A number of international helicopter records were established at an early stage, including a speed of 212mph over a three kilometre course. This helped to stimulate some export interest, with orders being received before it entered service with the French Navy. The first to place an order was Israel, which operated 12 in the airborne assault role. Further deliveries were made to Iran (16), Libya (9) and South Africa (16).*

In addition to the French production line, further examples of the Super Frelon have been built in China as the Z-8, under a licence agreement.

LEFT: *The Eurocopter Tiger has been designed to meet the requirement for an agile, all-weather, anti-tank combat helicopter for the French and German Armies. Originally designated PAH-2, the prototype first flew on 27th April 1991. Series production is planned to commence in 1997 and present planning is based on a requirement for 352 of the anti-tank version, which will be equipped with the HOT 2 and/or Trigat. These ATGMs will be fitted on the stub wings. This variant will also be fitted with the gyro-stabilized Mast Mounted Sight (MMS), which provides infra-red and TV pictures as well as a laser rangefinder and missile tracker. The German Tigers will be fitted with Stinger AAMs, while the French will have the Mistral for air-to-air attack or defence. The German requirement was for 212 Tigers, but recent defence cuts have required a substantial reduction.*

In addition, a further 75 Tigers configured for combat support are planned. These will be armed with rocket pods on the stub wings in addition to the 30mm cannon in the nose. Both variants will be provided with an advanced cockpit suite, which includes a helmet-mounted sight and display system.

RIGHT: *The Aerospatiale Dauphin has been developed as a single- and twin-engined replacement for the Alouette III. The single-seat SA.360 was first flown on 29th January 1973, and the twin-engined SA.365 on 24th January 1975. The military variants are capable of carrying 10 assault troops or can be used in the attack role with 8 HOT ATGW missiles or 20mm cannon, rockets, and 7.62mm machine gun.*

Naval variants have also been developed for ASW & ASV, for which it can be fitted with the AS.15TT air-to-surface missile as well as SAR.

Deliveries of the Dauphin have been made to Angola, Chile, Congo, Ivory Coast, Hong Kong, Ireland, Malawi and Saudi Arabia, as well as to the French Air Force and Navy and the US Coast Guard.

LEFT: *The Eurocopter AS565 Panther is a development of the of the Dauphin II which has been especially developed for the military market. The Panther is capable of carrying 12 troops in the support role as well as being fitted with gun and rocket pods. It is also has the capabilities of operating as an anti-surface vessel (ASV) or anti-submarine warfare (ASW) platform.*

It is in service with the French Navy.

ABOVE: The Eurocopter Fennec was originally known as the Ecureuil when it was designed and built by Aerospatiale. It was produced as the successor to the Alouette II and the prototype first flew on the 27th June 1974.

Besides serving with the French Armed services, military export customers for the Ecureuil/Fennec have included Australia, Comores, Djibouti, Guinea, Sierra Leone and Singapore. Brazil built a quantity under licence for their armed forces, where they are known locally as Esquilo.

The Danish Army purchased 12 Fennecs to provide it with its first airborne anti-tank capability. The first of these were delivered on 15th August 1990 and they are fitted with two double SAAB Emerson HeliTOW pods – one on either side.

RIGHT: The first Bolkow 105 took to the air on 16th February 1967. It is a highly manoeuvrable helicopter and is fitted with a rigid rotor which gives it full aerobatics capability. While a number are operated on the civilian market, by far the largest proportion of the Bo.105s built serve with military forces around the world.

The German Army has some 100 Bo.105Ms to replace the Alouette IIs in the observation and liaison role. In addition, 212 Bo.105Ps or PAH-1s serve in the anti-tank role, for which they are fitted with six HOT ATGMs.

RIGHT: The Bo.105 is now marketed under the Eurocopter label following the signing of a cooperation agreement between France and Germany. The Bo.105 has been widely sold throughout the world, examples having been supplied to Bahrain (3), Brawny (6), Chile (6), Lesotho (2), Mexico (12), Netherlands (31), Nigeria (4), Philippines (10), Sierra Leone (1), Spain (60+) and Sudan (12).

Production has also taken place in Indonesia for its civilian and military requirements.

In addition to these, the Royal Swedish Army took delivery of 20 Bo.105CBs (illustrated). This has a capacity for four to five persons for observation and communications but it is seen here fitted with the SAAB-Emerson HeliTOW ATGM for the anti-tank role. A further four Bo.105CBs are operated by the Swedish Air Force for SAR.

BELOW LEFT: The NH 90 is the result of a memorandum of understanding signed by the defence ministers of France, Germany, Italy, Netherlands and the UK for a new NATO Helicopter for the '90s (hence NH 90).

Two basic variants have been designed. The NFH 90 will be operated from frigates in the ASW, ASV and SAR roles. The TTH 90 will fly the tactical transport missions and will be able to carry 20 troops or a two-ton vehicle, for which access will be through a rear ramp. The UK withdrew from the programme in 1987 to proceed with the larger EH.101, although Italy, with Agusta, has remained in both.

The first flight of the NH 90 is planned for 1993, with the first deliveries being made in 1997. Approximately 600 are required by the participating nations.

INDEX

Picture Credits

CHRIS ALLAN: ½ title page; BOB ARCHER: 96(t), 100/101, 134(t), 134(b), 135(t), 135(m), 136(t), 136(mr); CHRIS BROOKS: 45(b); DENIS CALVERT: 22(b), 74(b); GRZEGORZ CZWARTOSZ: 37, 94(t), 191(t), 134(m), 137(t), 137(mu); JEREMY FLACK/ AVIATION PHOTOGRAPHS INTERNATIONAL: 4, 5, 6, 7, 8/9, 10, 13, 14(t), 14(m), 14(b), 15(t), 15(b), 16, 18, 19(t), 19(b), 20/21, 21(m), 21(b), 22(t), 23(m), 23(b), 23(t), 24(t), 25(t), 26, 27, 28(t), 28(b), 28/29, 29, 30(t), 30(b), 30/31, 31(t), 31(b), 32(m), 33(t), 33(m), 33(b), 34, 35(t), 35(b), 38(t), 38(b), 39(b), 40(t), 41(t), 44(t), 44(m), 44(b), 45(t), 48, 50, 51(t), 52(t), 53(b), 54(m), 54(b), 55(t), 55(m), 55(b), 58, 59(t), 59(b), 61(t), 61(m), 63(t), 63(bl), 65(m), 65(b), 66(t), 66(m), 67(t), 67(m), 68(t), 71(b), 72(b), 73(m), 73(b), 76/77(t), 81(t), 81(m), 83(t), 83(b), 84, 87(t), 98(t), 98(b), 99(m), 99(b), 102/103, 103(bl), 103(br) 105(m), 105(b), 107, 108(t), 109(t), 110(t), 110(b), 111(t), 112(t), 112(m), 113(t), 113(m), 113(bl), 113(br), 114(t), 114(b), 115(t), 115(m), 115(b), 116(t), 116(m), 116(b), 117(m), 117(b), 118(t), 118(b), 119(t), 119(m), 121(t), 122(t), 123(t), 124(t), 124(b), 125(b), 126(t), 126(mu), 126(ml), 128(t), 128(b), 130((t), 130(m), 130(b), 131(all), 136(ml), 137(ml), 137(b), 139(t); MIKE FREER: 58/59; GEOFF LEE/BRITISH AEROSPACE: 17, 20; TONY PAXTON: Title Page, 26/ 27, 32(t), 71(t); LINDSAY PEACOCK: 79(b), 95(b), 100(t); JOHN SHAKESPEARE: 120(b); ROBBIE SHAW: 16/17, 40(b), 43(t), 66(b), 67(b), 86, 122(b); PETER STEINEMANN/SKYLINE APA: 12/13, 24/5, 25(b), 39(t), 40(m), 41(m), 41(b), 42(t), 41(m), 41(b), 43(b), 51(m), 51(b), 52(m), 52(b), 59(m), 64(t), 64(b), 68(m), 76/77(b), 78, 78/79, 79(t), 80(m), 80(b), 81(b), 82(t), 87(b), 91(t), 91(b), 92(b), 93(t), 93(b), 95(t), 96(b), 97(t), 97(b), 98(t), 99(t), 99(inset), 125(t), 135(b), 136(b); STEVE WOLF: 88(t); AGUSTA: 133(t); ALENIA: 36; BELL: 129; BOEING: 119(b), 132(b); BULGARIAN AF: 102; CATIC: 133(b); DASSAULT AVIATION/AVIAPLANS: 84/85, 85; DEPARTMENT OF DEFENCE: 12, 32(b), 46(t), 46(b), 47(t), 47(b), 48/49(b), 50/51, 54(t), 56, 56/ 57, 58, 60, 61(b), 62(m), 62(b), 65(t), 68(b), 69(t), 69(b), 72(t), 88(b), 92(t), 93(m), 94(b), 95(m), 104(t), 104(b), 105(t), 106, 112(b), 117(t), 120(t), 121(b); EMBRAER: 36/37; EUROCOPTER: 109(b), 138(t), 138(m), 138(b), 139(mu), 139(ml), 139(b); GENERAL DYNAMICS: 48/49(t), 53(t); HUGHES: 62(t), 132(t); LOCKHEED: 11, 70; MCDONNELL DOUGLAS: 11, 72/72, 74(t), 75, 123(b); MITSUBISHI: 86; ROYAL NAVY: 111(b); SAAB: 89(t), 89(b), 90(t), 90(b); SIKORSKY: 127(t), 127(b); SIRPA AIR: 80(t), 82(b); VF-102: 61(br), 63; WESTLAND HELICOPTERS: 108(b), 126(b)